STORIED BARS
OF
New York

STORIED BARS
OF
New York

Where Literary Luminaries Go to Drink

DELIA CABE

The Countryman Press
A division of W. W. Norton & Company
Independent Publishers Since 1923

For information about special discounts for bulk purchases, please contact W. W. Norton Special Sales at specialsales@wwnorton.com or 800-233-4830

The Countryman Press
www.countrymanpress.com

A division of W. W. Norton & Company, Inc.
500 Fifth Avenue, New York, NY 10110
www.wwnorton.com

978-1-68268-046-9

10 9 8 7 6 5 4 3 2 1

For Rob

You're the Nick to my Nora

CONTENTS

East Village

McSorley's Old Ale House *83*

KGB Bar/The Red Room at KGB *89*
COCKTAIL:
Moscow Mule 94

Nuyorican Poets Cafe *97*
COCKTAIL:
Plum Daiquiri 99

Chelsea

Hotel Chelsea/El Quijote Restaurant *103*
COCKTAIL:
Gin-Tonic 109

The Half King Bar and Restaurant *111*
COCKTAIL:
Whiskey Caipirinha with Mint 114

Flatiron District/Gramercy Park

Old Town Bar *119*

Pete's Tavern *123*
COCKTAIL:
Frozen Strawberry Daiquiri 126

Bo's Kitchen & Bar Room *129*
COCKTAILS:
Julia's Glass 133
Serpent's Nectar 135

Midtown Manhattan

Upper East Side

Upper West Side

Brooklyn

Long Island City, Queens

"For one thing, I take New York personally. I am, in fact, somewhat annoyingly tender about it. A silver cord ties me tight to my city."

—DOROTHY PARKER

"My Home Town," *McCall's*, January 1928

INTRODUCTION

I grew up on the Lower East Side of Manhattan. A lifelong bookworm, I would often walk the streets of New York City imagining the many authors who had lived and written in the apartments I passed. My grade school on Christopher Street in Greenwich Village was located one block from the Lion's Head, a celebrated watering hole for writers and journalists. I knew E. E. Cummings, Dawn Powell, Thomas Paine, and Ted White had all lived on Christopher Street at one time or another. Dorothy Parker and I went to Catholic school in the same double brownstone on W. 79th Street in Manhattan, separated by numerous decades. Unlike the class troublemaker Dottie, I thrived in that brownstone, with its dark wood touches and a layout that I could imagine being someone's home. Had I been of legal age, I would have toasted Dorothy's ghost in my classroom with a tall glass of gin. Unfortunately, the only alcohol allowed was the red wine served at communion during mass in the first-floor chapel.

Once I was old enough, I had to check out the Algonquin Hotel, where the writers and artists of the Round Table met in the 1920s. To this day, the lobby and Blue Room bar, updated in 2012, attract authors and book lovers from the world over. The hotel and its bar are proud of their place in the annals of literature and endeavor to make their standing relevant in the twenty-first century. Often tourists in the know have their pictures taken beneath the painting of the Round Table members, while others are content to curl up with a book in a lobby chair, a Dorothy Parker cocktail at hand. I basked in the indigo glow of the Blue Room, a perpetual twilight atmosphere in which to imbibe a luscious cocktail. Hallowed ground, indeed.

But it's not just the glitzy spots that stand out. I've slipped into McSorley's for the requisite pair of mugs of beer and the walls covered with framed newspaper clippings, photos, and the book jacket from Joseph Mitchell's *McSorley's Wonderful Saloon*. The author's photo shows a gentle, balding man peering through large round glasses. Mitchell seems on the brink of a smile. Kettle of Fish, in the former home of the Lion's Head, feels comforting, unpretentious. The "21" is upscale but charming, its ceiling laden with toys, books, and playful memorabilia. You can almost picture Truman Capote, whose biography by George Plimpton dangles above the bar, regaling his table with his many tales.

This book is a collection of those storied bars that have played host to writers and artists for more than a century. A few of the bars spotlighted in this book have been pouring liquor for literary luminaries since Grover Cleveland was president. Yet, while New York City preserves and treasures parts of its past, the city also reinvents itself year after year. While every generation of writers injects the classic haunts with fresh energy, new bars appear on the scene ready to inherit a literary mantle, welcoming contemporary writers and readers into the fold. Watering holes like the Half King, KGB, LIC Bar, and Franklin

Park hold reading series showcasing best-selling and emerging authors. Overflowing audiences of book lovers, journalists, authors, and publishing industry types sit during the readings like worshippers in a temple. They return on other days for drinks, conversation, or some reading time. Franklin Park's outdoor patio provides a pocket of tranquility, where patrons lounge and read on a summer afternoon, away from the hectic Brooklyn streets. Gary Shteyngart, who enjoys this bar's reading series, however, prefers to drink his vodka and tonic at "clandestine downtown bars."

Myriad theories abound as to why writers congregate in bars. They patronize them because they are thirsty. They patronize them because they need a break from the solitary task of writing that novel, essay, magazine story, or poem. They patronize them looking for camaraderie. (And some patronized them far too often.)

The bars authors frequented and still do frequent have buoyed their creativity. Coffee shops may be their so-called third place by day, but these bars are their third place by night. Magazines such as *The New Yorker* and *Saturday Review* were conceived over drinks. Walt Whitman penned a few poems in a New York bar in the late nineteenth century. Mostly, he liked to sit back and observe the scene, listening to the cadence of conversations around him. O. Henry wrote his short story "The Gift of the Magi" at a Gramercy Park bar. Ludwig Bemelmans drafted his children's book on the back of a menu in that same bar. In a Manhattan bar, Thomas Wolfe discerned the central theme of the novel he was wrestling with when a drinking companion told the North Carolina native that you can't go home again. Edward Albee saw "Who's Afraid of Virginia Woolf" scrawled in soap on a bathroom mirror in a Greenwich Village bar and was inspired to write a Tony Award–winning play of the same name. More recently, Jay McInerney chose a Tribeca bar and restaurant for scenes in his novels *Bright Lights, Bright City* and *Bright, Precious Days* as recently as 2016.

No doubt, writers turn to these boîtes for friendship and conviviality because writing is a lonely endeavor. In bars old and new, they socialize, critique each other's works in progress, and connect each other to writing and teaching gigs, to residencies, retreats, and conferences, and to other writers, editors, and agents. That's true now, just as it was way back when.

Robert Sherwood shared an office with Robert Benchley and Dorothy Parker when all three were writing for *Vanity Fair*. "Ever since then, my considered advice to young literary aspirants has been, 'Merely make sure that you start out in fast company,'" Sherwood writes. After all, an impromptu luncheon of newspaper and magazine writers and editors, including those witty three, to celebrate Alexander Woollcott's return from World War I gave rise to the Round Table. They had steady writing assignments because of those lunches.

Journalists, photojournalists, and documentarians, Ernest Hemingway included, have always sought respite from the horrors of war in hotel and dive bars. In Chelsea, Sebastian Junger and two friends, a writer and a documentarian, opened the Half King seeking to replicate the overseas bars where they and other foreign correspondents found camaraderie. In their reading series, others can join in on the conversation on current events.

I would be remiss if I didn't acknowledge the toll alcoholism has taken on writers' lives. Too many literary lights, including Dorothy Parker, William Styron, E. E. Cummings, and F. Scott Fitzgerald, were dimmed because of booze. "Never did Dorothy appear drunk," Marion Meade writes. "But she was seldom completely sober." Parker sipped

Scotch throughout the day to calm her. Drink also put her in good spirits and loosened her up.

These writers suffered physically and mentally because of their addiction. In some instances, they were medicating themselves, looking to drive away the demons of depression, anxiety, and other mental anguish. When writer's block hit, the bottle became their muse. Sadly, that muse did not always lead to more words spilled on a page.

Charles Jackson, in his semi-autobiographical novel *The Lost Weekend*, portrays the five-day binge of an alcoholic writer in all its stark reality. Some scenes in his groundbreaking novel, the forerunner of contemporary addiction literature, take place in a bar like P.J. Clarke's, Jackson's own watering hole. Authors like Pete Hamill gave up alcohol when they recognized the havoc it had wreaked on their own lives. Hamill recounts his days and nights bookended by drink in his poignant yet raw memoir *A Drinking Life*.

And yet.

From Manhattan to Brooklyn to Queens, New York's literary community flourishes. After a day wrestling with prose and verse, they leave their writing, perhaps in mid-sentence as Hemingway allegedly did, and head for the bars. "But when evening quickens in the street, comes a pause in the day's occupation that is known as the cocktail hour," writes Bernard DeVoto in *The Hour: A Cocktail Manifesto*, first published in 1948. "It marks the lifeward turn." On any given night, author readings or open mic poetry slams are on tap in one or more bars in the city.

Come with me then, and follow in the boozy footsteps of legendary authors or make tracks to the newer literary hotspots.

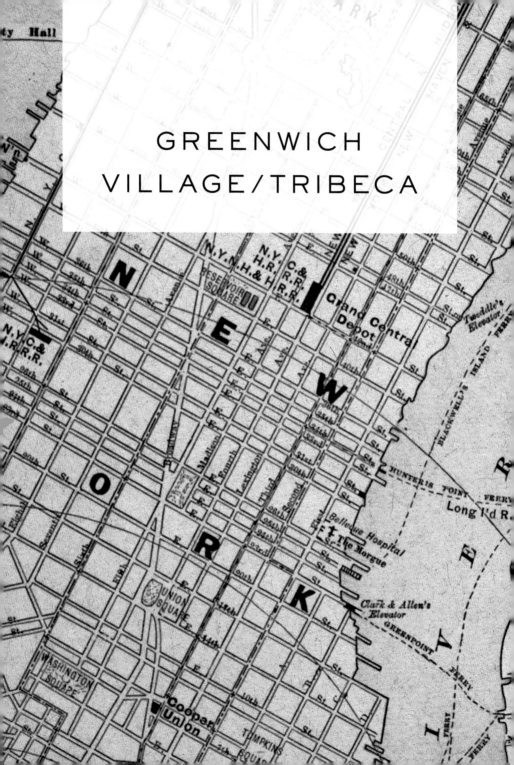

GREENWICH VILLAGE/TRIBECA

Once upon a time, when Greenwich Village offered inexpensive apartments, this area of Lower Manhattan was an enclave for parched journalists, novelists, and poets. The *WPA Guide to New York City*, published in 1939, describes the Village as "the center of the American Renaissance or of artiness" after World War I. But the Village's welcome mat for nonconformist characters was rolled out much earlier.

Because of its reputation, Thomas Paine—journalist, propagandist, and revolutionary—chose the Village as his home upon returning to America after spending some years in France, where he'd also served time in prison. In the late nineteenth century, other literary rebels, including Walt Whitman, were drawn to the Village and became America's first bohemians, congregating at a local saloon. The *WPA Guide* notes the number of "serious artists and writers," that is, "bohemians in renovated (carriage) houses," who had taken up residence in the Village. With so many writers in this one section of Manhattan, many literary journals, magazines, publishing houses, and newspapers sprung up in and on the periphery of the Village.

When they weren't writing and editing, they joined their fellow writers for a tipple or two or three or more at Village saloons, taverns, speakeasies—and then, post-Prohibition, legal watering holes. Later, the Beat writers occupied the stools and booths of these same bars as well as newer ones that embraced them.

Patti Smith, Pete Hamill, Caleb Carr, Maurice Sendak, and many other writers would soon join them in the coming decades.

Today, roam its idiosyncratic streets, alleys, and mews and spot numerous plaques commemorating places where famous authors lived and drank. After wandering the Village's streets and lanes tracing the steps of its writers, lucky bibliophiles can quench their thirst at the bars frequented by celebrated authors.

Pfaff's

647 BROADWAY
CLOSED

The story of the love affair between writers and New York's bars, taverns, pubs, and speakeasies begins in lower Manhattan in a nineteenth-century saloon. While the bar no longer exists, it holds a pivotal place in the annals of literary history—and drinking. Charles Ignatius Pfaff, a kindhearted, rotund man of German-Swiss descent with short, stiff hair, arrived in New York with dreams of owning a *rathskeller*, the German word for a tavern or bar located in a basement. Sometime in the late 1850s, he opened Pfaff's, which he advertised as a "restaurant and lager bier [*sic*] saloon," in the basement of a fine hotel near the corner of Bleecker Street, on the southeastern edge of what is now New York University. His subterranean establishment, in the heart of New York's then theater district and about a mile from Newspaper Row, where all city newspapers had offices, caught the eye of Henry Clapp Jr.

A Massachusetts native, Clapp founded the literary journal *Saturday Review*, a countercultural publication, in 1858 in Pfaff's. His newspaper, advertised as "a weekly journal of literary, artistic, dramatic, and music intelligence," was considered New York's answer to the *Atlantic Monthly*, a literary magazine started in Boston the year before. The newspaper was akin to the alternative weeklies found in urban areas today. "To the scholar, the literary man, and the man of taste, in all matters of art and literature, we consider this paper almost a necessity," a reviewer for the *Hartford Courant* wrote of Clapp's new publication.

Before Clapp settled in Manhattan, he had lived for a few years in France, where he had become smitten with the life of bohemians in Paris. Unlike members of the upper class, who held intellectual conversations in proper salons, these outcast artists and writers carried on their discussions in watering holes while swilling absinthe. Bohemians disdained bourgeois life, preferring a rakish existence marked by free thinking. Since Clapp's return to America, he had been looking to establish a bit of Bohemia in New York, and Pfaff's, in a prime location, had the right atmosphere.

Pfaff's offered excellent Rhine wines, liquor, German-style lager (served in steins) and pfannekuchen (German pancakes), beefsteak, cheese, and other edibles served on fine china with genuine silver flatware. The saloon, one of the few that welcomed women, was by no means genteel. Rough and tumble laborers, firemen, actors from nearby playhouses, newspapermen, and others filled its tables.

In this plain and quaint place, Clapp could realize his bohemian dream. He selected from his circle of literary friends, many of whom wrote for his own publication, as well as essayists, critics, journalists, playwrights, poets, actors, and artists to join him for conversation and drink. At the small tables, these working writers and artists could sit for hours imbibing alcohol or coffee in the gas-lit, smoke-filled basement, its floor covered with sawdust. While they all earned a living for the most part from their creative endeavors, they were paid little. Pfaff didn't think twice about putting a drink on a running tab if one of his patrons lacked cash or was between jobs.

Eventually, the saloonkeeper offered these American bohemians a long table in a cave-like area with a vaulted ceiling beneath the sidewalk, where they could hang out and hold forth on current events, women's rights, the abolitionist movement, politics, free love, religion, the human condition, their creative work. Puns, quips, and jokes were sprinkled throughout the conversation. They regaled each other with stories, at times humorous, at times bleak, and also brought in their works in progress for feedback. A contemporary wrote years later, "Those were merry and famous nights, and many bright conceits and witticisms were discharged over the festive board." Because of his dissolute life and dark tales, the recently deceased Edgar Allen Poe became the group's patron saint and the spiritual guide of Bohemia.

During the evenings, Clapp, christened the "King of Bohemia," sat at the head of the table and traded quips with 25 to 30 people.

On any given night, those joining him might include the actresses and writers, Ada Clare (known as "Queen of Bohemia") and Adah Isaacs Menken (a brandy-swigging cigar smoker), actor Edwin Booth (his brother John Wilkes Booth assassinated Abraham Lincoln), writer Fitz-James O'Brien, artist Winslow Homer, and *New York Tribune* publisher Horace Greeley. Of Greeley, Clapp jibed, "Horace is a self-made man, and he worships his creator." Greeley took this jibe, one of Clapp's many famous taunts, in stride. A statue of Greeley, seated in a bronze reading chair with newspaper in hand, resides in the northeast corner of City Hall Park today. The saloonkeeper had a seat at their table, too, because he loved his regulars, these American bohemians.

By 1859, Walt Whitman joined the group, traveling by ferry from his Brooklyn home. He was 39 years old, a soon-to-be out-of-work newspaperman with a book of poetry called *Leaves of Grass*, written in nontraditional verse. His book was not selling well. Within a short period, Whitman was part of the inner circle and a habitué. "I used to go to Pfaff's every night," the Good Gray Poet told a reporter for *The Brooklyn Daily Eagle* in 1866. "It used to be a pleasant place to go in the evening after taking a bath and finishing a day of work." Whitman disliked Pfaff, the saloonkeeper, the first time they met. "But my subsequent acquaintance with him taught me not to be too hasty in making up my mind about people on first sight. . . . He was always kind to beggars and gave them food freely. Then he was easily moved to sympathize with anyone who was in trouble and was generous with his money. I believe he was at that time the best judge of wine of anybody in this country."

Whitman, in his large felt hat, baggy pants, and his tousled hair and beard, liked the "convivial coteries of Bohemia" congregating at Pfaff's, sometimes writing while sitting there, imbibing little. Perhaps he sipped a glass of port or gin cocktails, both of which he claimed aided the writing of his temperance novel, *Franklin Evans, or The Inebriate: A Tale of the Times,* in the early 1840s. "My own greatest pleasure at Pfaff's was to look on—to see, talk little, absorb. I never was a great discusser, anyway—never. I was much better satisfied to listen to a fight than take part in it," he said. Despite his reticence, he drew many people to him. William Dean Howells, author of the novel *The Rise of Silas Lapham,* first met Whitman at Pfaff's and wrote that Whitman, "the apostle of the rough, the uncouth, was the gentlest person."

Homosexuals also felt at ease at Pfaff's, and Whitman's homosexuality was no secret within its subterranean walls. Whitman was part of a group of men that called themselves the "Fred Gray Association" and explored the idea of same-sex romance. Whitman may have first met Frederick Vaughan, an Irish-Canadian stagecoach driver, there one evening. The two embarked on a romantic relationship. (The relationship ended because of Vaughan's excessive drinking. Vaughan later married a woman.)

During the day, Whitman sometimes visited the sick and injured patients at New York Hospital. When he was done, he'd invite the staff to join him for beers and frankfurters at Pfaff's. When Ralph Waldo Emerson visited New York, he met up with Whitman, who had sent him an early draft of *Leaves of Grass*. Emerson had been impressed with Whitman's poems. Whitman took him to Pfaff's to introduce the Boston transcendentalist around to his bohemian friends.

Clapp, meanwhile, became Whitman's literary champion. He published poems from Whitman's *Leaves of Grass* in the *Saturday Review*. He printed the good and the bad reviews of Whitman's collection, figuring that even a bad review was good publicity for the book. He sought advertisements from the printer of Whitman's third edition of *Leaves of Grass*. Whitman credited Clapp with helping him establish his career as a poet. (Clapp also was the first to publish a short story by Mark Twain, "Jim Smiley and His Jumping Frog," later renamed "The Celebrated Frog of Calaveras County.")

At the start of the Civil War, the group scattered. They supported the Union and were abolitionists, but few were young or healthy enough to enlist in the Union Army. Whitman went to Washington, DC, where he cared for wounded soldiers in Union Army hospitals. He corresponded with his friends at Pfaff's. Clapp, the oldest of the group, stayed behind.

Clapp became a heavy drinker when his resurrected *Saturday Review* failed. He wandered the streets of Manhattan, penniless, homeless, destitute, between stints in asylums. Upon his death in 1875, an obituary in *The New York Times* stated "no man was better known in the newspaper and artistic world a few years ago than the eccentric and gifted King of the Bohemians."

After several years in Washington, Whitman moved to Camden, New Jersey. In 1881, he stopped by Pfaff's, which had since moved uptown to 9 W. 24th Street, for the last time, and he and Pfaff reminisced about those Bohemian evenings. In 1888, Whitman suffered a paralytic stroke, and he died of pneumonia in 1892.

One of the unfinished poems found in his notebooks is called "The Two Vaults." This draft was written in the early 1860s:

> The vault at Pfaffs where the drinkers and laughers meet to eat and
> drink and carouse
> While on the walk immediately overhead pass the myriad feet of
> Broadway
> As the dead in their graves are underfoot hidden
> And the living pass over them, recking not of them,
> Laugh on laughers!
> Drink on drinkers!
> Bandy the jest!
> Toss the theme from one to another!
> Beam up—Brighten up, bright eyes of beautiful young men!
> Eat what you, having ordered, are pleased to see placed before you—
> after the work of the day, now, with appetite eat,
> Drink wine—drink beer—raise your voice,
> Behold! your friend, as he arrives—Welcome him, where, from the
> upper step, he looks down upon you with a cheerful look
> Overhead rolls Broadway—the myriad rushing Broadway
> The lamps are lit—the shops blaze—the fabrics vividly are seen through the
> plate glass windows
> The strong lights from above pour down upon them and are shed outside,

The thick crowds, well-dressed—the continual crowds as if they would
never end
The curious appearance of the faces—the glimpse just caught of the eyes
and expressions, as they flit along,
(You phantoms! oft I pause, yearning, to arrest some one of you!
Oft I doubt your reality—whether you are real—I suspect all is but a
pageant.)
The lights beam in the first vault—but the other is entirely dark
In the first

Forced to close his saloon because of financial difficulties, Charles Pfaff retired in 1887. The original building on 647 Broadway still stands. The cellar is used by the store above it for storage. Whitman once observed, "Bohemia comes but once in one's life. Let's treasure even its memory."

In 2011, a restaurateur sought to capitalize on a part of New York history and opened a place called The Vault at Pfaff's at 643 Broadway, a few doors down from the original. The cellar bar was designed to evoke a speakeasy, albeit an upscale one. The menu resembled vintage newspapers. Cocktails gave a nod to Pfaff's original denizens with names like Leaves of Grass, Ada Clare, The Pfapple, and Bohemian. It closed two years later. Now the subterranean space is home to a bar called Sweetwater Social, where customers can choose from seasonal cocktails and play vintage arcade games.

The legacy and spirit that originated at Pfaff's lives on elsewhere. Raise your glass to the American bohemians. Drink on drinkers! Bandy the jest!

LEAVES OF GRASS

Recipe courtesy of Frank Caiafa

Whether any cocktails were served at Pfaff's is knowledge that has been lost to the ages, but Frank Caiafa consulted the history of Pfaff's when he was brought in to oversee the cocktail program of the reincarnated Vault at Pfaff's. The award-winning mixologist embarked on extensive research for the Vault cocktail menu. His Walt Whitman-inspired cocktail makes inventive use of port, a dessert wine Whitman alleged helped him write his novel.

Leaves of Grass is offered on the cocktail menu of the celebrated Peacock Alley, a lounge and restaurant where Caiafa is the beverage director, at the Waldorf Astoria. Peacock Alley takes its name from the Waldorf Astoria's illustrious 300-foot corridor, where on Sundays affluent guests once strutted through in their gowns made by the finest dressmakers in the 1890s.

Besides being a master mixologist, Caiafa is an author. He revised and combined the Waldorf's proprietary classic cocktail books, *Old Waldorf Bar Days* (1931) and *Old Waldorf Astoria Bar Book* (1934), to produce *The Waldorf Astoria Bar Book*, which was published in 2016.

INGREDIENTS

2 ounces Żubrówka Bison Grass Vodka

¾ ounce Quinta do Noval 10 Year Old Tawny Port

½ ounce honey syrup[*]

¼ ounce fresh lemon juice

DIRECTIONS

Add ingredients to an ice-filled cocktail shaker. Shake well. Strain into chilled cocktail glass. Garnish with one blade of bison grass.

*HONEY SYRUP

INGREDIENTS

6 ounces honey

4 ounces water

DIRECTIONS

Add ingredients to saucepan and stir over medium heat until honey is dissolved. Remove from heat, let cool, and store in clean glass bottle. Refrigerate up to two months.

Minetta Tavern and Restaurant

113 MacDougal Street (between Bleecker and West 3rd)
minettatavernny.com
212-475-3850
Lunch: 12 to 3 p.m. (Wednesday through Friday)
Brunch: 11 a.m. to 3 p.m. (Saturday and Sunday)
Dinner: 5:30 p.m. to 12 a.m. (Sunday through Wednesday),
5:30 p.m. to 1 a.m. (Thursday through Saturday)

Wandering the streets of Greenwich Village in the early twentieth century was Joseph Ferdinand Gould: bohemian, beatnik poet, panhandler, Harvard Class of 1911, he stood about 5 feet, 4 inches and weighed less than 100 pounds. The poet Max Bodenheim described Joe Gould "with his tonsured head, piebald ecclesiastical beard, and bent shrunken frame . . . like a fugitive from a medieval monastery." Gould, nicknamed "Professor Sea Gull" because he mimicked the flapping bird and purported to speak "sea gull," the bird's language, told anyone who listened that he was writing "An Oral History of Our Times." In his black marbled composition books, using fountain pens filled with ink filched from the post office, he recorded snippets of conversation he overheard verbatim.

His days and nights were spent dealing with, in his phrase, "the three Hs": homelessness, hunger, and hangovers.

When Gould, a Massachusetts native with his Harvard University accent, arrived in New York in 1916, he worked as a reporter and published some of his writings in literary journals, until mental illness emerged. He was bright and eccentric, and in her biography *Joe Gould's Teeth*, author Jill Lepore suggests that he suffered from hypergraphia, a condition typified by a compulsion to write. Gould, along with several bohemian writers, became a denizen of Minetta Tavern, or simply "Minetta's," which opened in 1937.

Before that, a speakeasy, The Black Rabbit, occupied this corner until 1929. The founders of *Reader's Digest* worked out of the building's basement in the 1920s.

When it became Minetta Tavern (named for Minetta Brook, which crisscrossed the eponymous lane), E. E. Cummings, who lived on a gated cul-de-sac nearby, became a regular as well as one of Gould's many protectors. Cummings had known Gould from their Harvard days. After they reconnected in Manhattan, Cummings wrote a few poems that mention Gould. Cummings gave Gould clothing he no longer used and pocket money. He vouched for Gould when he was committed to a psychiatric hospital.

At age 20, William Saroyan read one of Gould's essays in the journal *The Dial*, later crediting it with freeing his own writing from form. When Saroyan learned years later who Gould was, he wrote a review of the piece. Upon hearing that, Gould showed up at Saroyan's Central Park South apartment building to see if his "literary disciple" might buy the toothless Gould a set of false teeth. The two went to a bar several times. Whether Saroyan picked up the tab on the dentures is not known; what is known is that Gould lost every set he procured. Cummings and Saroyan were among the writers who tried to convince editors to publish portions of his Oral History. A few appeared in print.

Gould would recite one of his poems at Minetta's, at a party with authors present, or on the street. He might perform the following and expect a thank you—a.k.a. money or a meal—in return:

My love for you is of the very cleanest;
Holy and sweet is my emotion.
There should be something deep between us,
And I suggest the Atlantic Ocean.

Or,

In winter I'm a Buddhist,
And in summer I'm a nudist.

In the early forties, *New Yorker* writer Joseph Mitchell became intrigued with Gould, spending hours with him. By then, Gould's Oral History was 26 years in the making, coming in at an estimated billion words. Mitchell's profile, "Professor Sea Gull," appeared in the December 12, 1942, edition of the magazine. With its publication, Gould, the self-proclaimed last bohemian, became a celebrity, receiving many letters, some with money. On the street, passersby would recognize him, stopping to talk to him.

Seeing an opportunity, the then owner of Minetta's asked Gould to come in nightly, as Gould could attract tourists hoping to see a genuine bohemian. For his labors as a tourist attraction, Gould received free meals. "I sit at a table in there from late in the afternoon until around 9, 10, or 11 at night and work on the Oral History and give some Village

atmosphere to the place. I am the resident bohemian, the house bohemian," Gould told Mitchell, who wrote a follow-up profile, "Joe Gould's Secret," in 1964.

Gould sat at prominent table in the front near a window, visible to tourists who passed by on Minetta Lane. Gould told women that if they kissed his bald spot, their dates had to buy him a drink. People bought him beer or wine—"If my need is great a martini," Gould said. He was partial to double martinis, which he downed during his meetings with Mitchell. Despite Gould's tattered grease/dirt/beer–stained clothing, his scraggly hair, and his resident lice, on a good evening, his bald pate would be covered with lipstick imprints. In one photo, Gould is shown being interviewed by gossip columnist Hedda Hopper.

As for Gould's secret? Gould died in 1957. Mitchell revealed in his second piece that the Oral History didn't exist. Gould had been rewriting the same few chapters all those years.

Mitchell, meanwhile, never published another piece after "Joe Gould's Secret." Until his death in 1996, he returned daily to the *New Yorker* offices in midtown, working behind closed doors. His was a famous case of writer's block that may or may not have been partly due to his relationship with Gould.

Today, Minetta's retains its original unassuming exterior, from the neon sign hanging above its corner entrance to the polished, salmon-colored slab at its front entrance with "Minetta's" in bronze script. Even MacDougall Street itself retains some of its bohemian/beatnik vibe from decades past. Bars, pizza shops, tattoo parlors, and coffee shops sit on the lower and street levels of old four- and five-story brick buildings, with fire escapes zigzagging down the front. The sushi shops and hipster barbecue places, however, will remind you that you are in the twenty-first century. But walking the length of MacDougal will give you a sense of its bygone era. Minetta's existence, along with Cafe Wha? across the street and the former site of San Remo's on the other end of the block, bookend the street's past. (Cafe Wha? is where Bob Dylan debuted, and it has also featured other young unknowns like Bruce Springsteen and Jimi Hendrix. Mary Travers waitressed there before she became a part of Peter, Paul, and Mary. See next entry for San Remo.)

Minetta Tavern's current owner, Keith McNally, bought the property in 2008. He had it renovated, with an eye toward an updated, yet nostalgic, classic look. He preserved Minetta's character and bones, including the refinished oak bar, tin ceiling, white subway tile, tobacco-smoke–stained murals depicting Greenwich Village history in the back dining room, framed caricatures of celebrities (drawn by abstract expressionist

Franz Kline for money), and photographs of such boxing greats as Rocky Graziano and Floyd Patterson mounted on the dark wainscoting. In keeping with its retro look, the old flooring was switched out for new black and white tile. Red banquettes line the exterior walls. Despite the crisp white table linens draping the dining tables, Minetta's feels like a cozy old-style bar up front with an intimate dining area in back.

Other writers who frequented Minetta's were Ernest Hemingway, Dylan Thomas, Eugene O'Neill, William Burroughs, and Ezra Pound. These days, you might spot Jay McInerney, Malcolm Gladwell, or *Vogue* editor Anna Wintour.

RHUBARB SOPHIE

Recipe courtesy of Minetta Tavern

Step aside, strawberry-rhubarb pie. Rhubarb, in the form of bitters, has joined the cocktail scene. The Michelin-starred Minetta Tavern has elevated the humble, bitter stalk with this mouth-watering cocktail. Each evening, the bartenders whip up this signature cocktail many times. The menu (be sure to order the Black Label burger) has been upgraded from the so-so Italian food of Joe Gould's days to food with a hint of a French accent. You could order a martini, but try the Rhubarb Sophie instead.

INGREDIENTS

2 cucumber slices

2 ounces vodka

1 ounce agave nectar

1 ounce fresh lime juice

2 dashes rhubarb bitters

DIRECTIONS

Muddle one cucumber slice in a shaker glass, then add the remaining ingredients along with ice. Shake vigorously for about 10 seconds. Strain into an ice-filled, double-rocks glass. Garnish with a slice of cucumber.

San Remo Café

189 Bleecker Street/93 MacDougal Street
Closed

A bronze plaque marks the site of the San Remo, now a coffee and tea shop, on the corner opposite from Minetta Tavern, where Bleecker intersects with MacDougal. The historic marker, mounted on the MacDougal side in 2013, lists ten of the literary and artistic icons who were regulars. The San Remo Café, an Italian-American coffeehouse that was more like a bar and restaurant, opened in 1925. When Prohibition ended in 1933, the bohemians flocked there to drink legally. Remo became the epicenter for the Beatniks after World War II. Their goings-on at this bar have become the stuff of literary legend. (*San Francisco Chronicle* columnist Herb Caen coined the term "beatnik," appending "nik," a Russian suffix, in 1958, six months after the Soviet satellite Sputnik was launched.)

Michael Harrington made the Remo his home for about a year in the fifties. "The Remo was a sort of Village United Nations," he wrote in *The Village Voice* in 1971. "It was straight and gay; black, white, and interracial; socialist, communist, Trotskyist, liberal, and apolitical; literary, religious, pot smoking, pill popping, and even occasionally transvestite." He called it "our Deux Magots," referring to the Parisian cafe where intellectuals, members of the Lost Generation, and artists socialized and drank.

Black-and-white photos by famed photographer Weegee show men in jackets and ties and women in fine hats and dresses crowded around its tables, drinking beer from bottles at the bar, leaning on the bar next to a tall, elaborate espresso machine from Italy (allegedly the first in the city). In one photo taken by Allen Ginsberg, William S. Burroughs, wearing a double-breasted suit, smokes a cigarette with poet and playwright Alan Ansen at the cafe's entrance. Ansen inspired outrageous characters in novels by Jack Kerouac, William S. Burroughs, and Gregory Corso.

In 1947, William Styron, newly arrived in the city for his job as a junior editor at McGraw-Hill, frequented the bar, an escape from his shabby apartment building on W. 11th Street. In the 1940s and 1950s, James Agee, who lived on the top floor of 172 Bleecker, preferred to sit alone, drinking heavily. Other literary lions who made the Remo their way-station included James Baldwin, Anatole Broyard, Dorothy Day, William Gaddis, Norman Mailer, Frank O'Hara, and Tennessee Williams.

Beat poet Gregory Corso, who was born in an apartment above a funeral parlor across the street at 190 Bleecker Street in 1930, made it one of his hangouts, as did fellow Beats Burroughs, Ginsberg, and Kerouac. Ginsberg first met Dylan Thomas at the Remo. Kerouac's *The Subterraneans* (another term for the Beatniks) is a semi-autobiographical novella that features a bar called the Black Mask based on the Remo. In his novel, Kerouac depicts the crowd as "hip without being slick, intelligent without being corny, they are intellectuals." The novel also describes a one-night stand between two men. And it was true.

In August 1953, a 28-year-old Gore Vidal and Kerouac, then 31, were drunk after a night of bar-hopping that began at the Remo. They checked into a room at the Chelsea Hotel under their own names, Vidal telling the clerk that the signed hotel register would be a keeper. "We owed it to literary history to couple," Vidal recalls in his memoir *Palimpsest*. Kerouac, in a kiss-and-tell move, announced the news of their tryst to a crowd at the Remo.

When Kerouac's *On the Road* was published in 1957 and brought him success, he felt wary in public. By then, he was living in Florida. He stopped in at the Remo, where three men beat him up outside.

Poet/novelist Maxwell Bodenheim was another familiar face, albeit disheveled and scraggly, at the Remo. He left Chicago, where he had

This plaque marks the spot where the San Remo once stood.

co-founded an irreverent journal, for the Village in the twenties. He wrote best-selling potboilers until he and his publisher were charged with producing indecent literature, specifically the book *Naked on Roller Skates*. The charge was dropped. He went on to face money troubles and became an alcoholic.

In February 1952, *Time* reported that Bodenheim, "one of the old breed of Greenwich Village Bohemians," was jailed for a day when he and six other "disheveled bums" were found snoozing on an empty train. Apparently, Bodenheim had been on a bender that night. After a friend posted the $25 bail, Bodenheim returned to the Remo.

Bodenheim would run into his fellow Village vagabond and rival, Joe Gould, at the bar. The two frequently argued and criticized each other's writings and life of eccentric vagrancy. Bodenheim would yell at his bar mates, in a voice tinged with his Mississippi roots, "I have a malady of the soul," or mumble, "Greenwich Village is the Coney Island of the soul." To the person who picked up his tab, he'd say, "I am a scarecrow body and a dead soul." Bodenheim wrote doggerel on napkins, selling them to tourists for 25 cents.

Bodenheim was shot to death in 1954. His murderer covered the bullet hole with a copy of Rachel Carson's *The Sea Around Us* that he found in the apartment. The next day at the Remo, caricaturist Jake Spencer slammed the poet's favorite gin glass on the tile floor and offered a toast: "Max was a splendid type. He used to write poetry in a booth here and then try to peddle the verse at the bar for a drink of gin," *Time* reported.

Most of the Beats dispersed around the country. In the sixties, Remo was known as a gay bar and was a favorite of Andy Warhol's.

The San Remo served its last drink in 1967.

BEATNIK

Spirits writer Duggan McDonnell created this cocktail, a Manhattan made over, in tribute to the Beat Generation's ties to his hometown, San Francisco, where he has worked as a bartender. Herb Caen, a lauded columnist of the *San Francisco Chronicle*, bestowed the Beats with this nickname in a 1958 column.

INGREDIENTS

1½ ounces Averna Amaro
1 ounce bourbon
½ ounce tawny or ruby port
1 dash Peychaud's bitters
Orange twist

DIRECTIONS

Add the Averna, bourbon, and bitters to a mixing glass filled with ice. Rinse the cocktail glass with port, and pour the port into the mixing glass. Stir well. Strain into the cocktail glass. Holding the orange peel colored side down, squeeze the orange peel as you draw it slowly over a lit match or lighter to lightly caramelize the oils. Garnish with a flamed orange twist.

Kettle of Fish/ Lion's Head

59 Christopher Street (cross streets: 7th Avenue South and W. 4th Street)
kettleoffishnyc.com
212-414-2278
Monday through Friday: 3 p.m. to 4 a.m.
Saturday and Sunday: 2 p.m. to 4 a.m.

Take three steps down into Kettle of Fish, where two literary bars merge in one dark basement bar. Kettle of Fish and Lion's Head began their lives on separate streets in Greenwich Village. For 30 years, Lion's Head served a veritable who's who of writers, journalists, editors, and newspaper photographers on Christopher Street until its closing in 1996. (Christopher Street, among the oldest streets in the Village, was home to Thomas Paine, E. E. Cummings, Harlan Ellison, and Dawn Powell.) Another venerable Village bar for writers, Kettle of Fish relocated its bar from W. 3rd Street to this location and took up the Lion's Head's mantle in 1999. Sort of.

Let's begin with the history of the Head, as it was called by the regulars. The Head was first a coffee bar at Hudson and Perry Streets until

1966, when John Wesley Joice bought it, obtained a liquor license, and moved the Head into a former doctor's office on Christopher Street. Joice was an ex-cop, an ex-bartender at P.J. Clarke's, and a voracious reader. Next door, *The Village Voice* had settled in on the same Christopher Street block in the sixties. The newspaper, co-founded by Norman Mailer, has published a wonderful roster of writers: James Baldwin, Lester Bangs, E. E. Cummings, Allen Ginsberg, Pete Hamill, Nat Hentoff, Katherine Ann Porter, Ezra Pound, and Tom Stoppard, to name a few.

The Head became a home away from home for the *Voice*'s ink-stained wretches. When the *Voice* staff tired of composing stories hunched over their typewriters and its copyeditors went bleary-eyed from correcting those stories, they wandered in, sometimes as early as the afternoon. Once the *Voice* writers realized that the new bar was owned by the well-read Joice, they brought their writer friends, even ones from rival publications.

Journalist-author Claudia Dreifus first frequented the Head while a student at New York University in the sixties. Dreifus considered the Head "the neighborhood dining room," akin to an Irish pub. In fact, the Clancy Brothers broke out into song whenever they dropped in. "You had a crowd, sort of a moveable feast," Dreifus recalls. "There was just a lot of companionship." If she arrived and didn't spot any familiar faces, she slipped into an empty chair at a table with others, making quick friends.

Hamill writes in his memoir *A Drinking Life*, "I don't think many New York bars ever had such a glorious mixture of newspapermen, painters, musicians, seamen, ex-communists, priests and nuns, athletes, stockbrokers, politicians, and folksingers, bound together in the leveling democracy of drink."

As unknown writers became book authors, they affixed their book covers to the walls, the first being *A Fan's Notes* by Fred Exley. At first, Joice, feigning irritation, asked them to stop using his tape. But the reader in him couldn't resist. The book jackets, in frames, were screwed into the walls to prevent theft. "The Wall was magnificent," Colum McCann told the magazine *Irish America*. McCann checked out the bar when he arrived from Dublin at age 17, because an editor told him the Head was a writer's hangout. "I wandered around and looked at all those wonderful book covers, some old and dusty, some brand spanking new. They were a novel in themselves. Therein lay a sense of creation." He promised himself that he would return one day when he had the "right to be there," on a barstool and on the wall. The cover of Dreifus's first book joined The Wall in the early seventies. Frank McCourt visited the bar while still a schoolteacher. Years later, his memoir *Angela's Ashes* gained him a spot. McCourt deemed that honor better than winning a Nobel Prize.

The bar attracted additional literati. James Baldwin observed that the Head "felt like the old days." Seamus Heaney and Jon Montague stopped in. Lanford Wilson used bar napkins to write a play while sitting there.

When a tourist stopped in to ask if this bar was where writers drank, Joice's wife, Judy, replied that it was patronized not by writers with drinking problems, but drinkers with writing problems.

Over the years, the food quality varied, depending on the culinary talents of the latest cook. At a 1986 reunion, Hamill told a *New York Times* reporter, "In the old days we had to leave to eat, and the telling thing was the owners went with us." *New Yorker* writer Tad Friend, who lived around the corner in the eighties and nineties, loved the Head. "It was great for a greasy cheeseburger and a beer and being left alone," he says.

Bankruptcy and high rents forced the Head to close in 1996. Adam Rogers, a science journalist and editor, was visiting New York, when a friend offered to take him to the bar where real reporters hung out. They walked past the Stonewall Inn, the birthplace of the gay rights movement and now a national monument, to a vacant Lion's Head. "I definitely missed joining a particular fraternity. I would have ordered whiskey," says Rogers, author of *Proof: The Science of Booze*.

In 1998, Patrick Daley, looking for a new spot for his bar, Kettle of Fish, took a look at the vacant space, and the bones of the place felt right.

Kettle of Fish started out on MacDougal Street in 1950 above the Gaslight Poetry Cafe (Max Bodenheim went there when it was a speakeasy). In its first decade, Beat poets would perform at the Gaslight and slake their thirst at the Kettle. Its neon sign "BAR" gained immortality when Jack Kerouac, his rumpled white shirt with its sleeves rolled up and its pocket sagging with a pack of cigarettes, posed for a color photo in front of it. This iconic photo, which also shows his girlfriend, Joyce Johnson, then an aspiring novelist who was working at a literary agency, was featured in Gap ads in the nineties.

Years later, when the Gaslight had given way to folksingers, they too would stop in between sets for a mug of 35-cent beer (30 cents before 6 p.m.) or a nosh. From a 1965 guidebook: "The somewhat older hipster—who's been around awhile and knows the scenes—migrates here several times a week to chart vibrations."

In 1981, Daley arrived in New York from his native Wisconsin, fell in love with Manhattan, and, as a regular, joined the Kettle's softball team. In 1983, he took up his position behind the bar. In 1986, when the Kettle relocated to W. 3rd Street, he went with it. In 1998, Daley bought

the name from his boss, who was retiring, and moved it to its current location. "I love this Kettle," he says. "It's closer to the original, has more of the original feel."

When Daley found the old Lion's Head sign in the basement, he mounted it on the left wall of the vestibule. A carved wooden fish serves as a door handle. The bar occupies the first room, while the adjacent room contains a sofa, dartboards, a pinball machine, and a bookcase with some books. As with the bar's previous incarnations, the paneled walls are covered with old photos of the Beats and other patrons. Behind the bar is a small box containing the ashes of Daley's best friend, John. Actually only about a teaspoonful remains—Daley dispersed the rest in Wisconsin.

The kitchen no longer exists. The only time Daley serves food is when his beloved Green Bay Packers have a football game. That's when his Wisconsin accent is at its most pronounced. During the game, Daley feeds a crowd of transplanted Wisconsin natives, also fervent Packers fans, a menu of cheese, bratwurst, summer sausage, and smoked chubs—all from their home state—served on paper plates. On other days, patrons may order in food from other establishments or bring in takeout. The bar is a no-frills beer and cocktails place that exudes warmth.

Like the Head's patrons, these bar-goers are there for camaraderie and for the annual Christmas carol sing-alongs, pumpkin-carving contests, and outings to see the Milwaukee Brewers play the New York Mets.

Readers and writers, fear not. Kettle of Fish, despite the numerous Packers and Wisconsin tchotchkes throughout, is not a sports bar. "Some people come here to write, nostalgic for its past," Daley says. But he believes in perpetuating the bar's bookish side. On one wall is a photo of Gregory Corso taken by Allen Ginsberg. "I threw out Gregory several times," Daley recalls. "He would imbibe too much rum and Coke." For several years, a group of writers met regularly to read aloud excerpts of their works in progress and to provide feedback. A Beats scholar has given a talk at the bar.

In 2016, a bartender and a regular patron started the Kettle Book Club, which meets about every six weeks. The first book the group tackled was Hamill's memoir *A Drinking Life*. They've also discussed Patti Smith's memoir *M Train* and novels by Anthony Doerr, Andre Dubus, and David Rakoff. You might even spot Dermot McEvoy and Michael Coffey, writers and Lion's Head regulars, having a drink.

And if you want to pose for a selfie with the iconic neon sign, head to the back room. The sign is displayed in the far corner, fully lit as it was the night of Kerouac's famous photo series. And yes, the bar does have an original print of the photo on one wall. "I feel like we're keeping a little part of old school New York alive," Daley says. Given the bar's various events, however, the Kettle feels more like a thriving Greenwich Village institution than a museum.

White Horse Tavern

567 Hudson Street (cross street: W. 11th Street)
212-989-3956
Sunday through Thursday: 11 a.m. to 1:30 a.m.
Friday and Saturday: 11 a.m. to 3:30 a.m.

Dylan Thomas looms large in White Horse Tavern. An entire room in this bar, established in 1880, the same year construction began on the Panama Canal, is dedicated to the Welsh poet, who had the last drinks of his life here. An imposing painting, based on a black-and-white photo, covers two-thirds of the height of one wall. Thomas, his forearms resting on the end of the bar, his hands enclosing a ceramic stein, stares out at the viewer. In turn, he seems to be looking at anyone who enters his room, his tavern.

Before Thomas and other writers anointed it, this watering hole was frequented by dock workers, laborers, and locals. After the White Horse waited out Prohibition as a speakeasy, it resumed serving alcohol legally in December 1933. In the forties, the White Horse, on the ground floor of a wood-framed building—a rarity in Manhattan—joined the chain of literary hangouts dotting Greenwich Village, the West Village, and Chelsea. Since then, several generations of writers have occupied its stools and held forth at its tables. Dan Wakefield, in his memoir *New York in the 50s*, observes, "For writers, the one place where you could always find a friend, join a conversation, relax and feel you were a part of a community was the White Horse."

In 1950, Thomas traveled to the United States for the first time to give about 40 readings, the initial one in New York. His tour was arranged by poet and literary critic John Malcolm Brinnin, who was then the director of what is now called the 92nd Street Y. During his stay, Brinnin and Scottish poet Ruthven Todd took Thomas to the tavern because its atmosphere was reminiscent of the pubs in Wales and Scotland.

Thomas, by then an alcoholic, became a sort of poet in residence at the place he called "the Horse." He attracted crowds, told yarns, and recited poems. On occasion, Thomas popped in at the San Remo, where he first met Allen Ginsberg, but the White Horse became his preferred bar. The San Remo crowd, he felt, with its beatniks, was too intellectual. When he returned to New York in 1952 and again in 1953, he'd spend hours here, starting with a late breakfast and beer. In his room at the White Horse hangs the original poster for his play *Under Milk Wood*, which had its New York debut in April 1953.

When Thomas, in his bedraggled suit and untidy hair, held court here, he could be captivating or rude, erudite or offensive. Oscar Williams, an editor of several major poetry anthologies, took the Village's bohemian vagrant Max Bodenheim to the White Horse to meet Thomas, a fellow recipient of an award from the magazine *Poetry*. The two knew little about each other. Thomas is said to have used his handkerchief to wipe Bodenheim's nose during their conversation.

His health in serious decline, Thomas returned to New York for the last time in October 1953, where he roomed at the Hotel Chelsea. Before

Poet Dylan Thomas is commemorated on the wall of the bar.

the trip, Thomas had suffered a few blackouts and had a chest ailment. New York's heavy smog aggravated his breathing difficulties. He participated in a few readings and a symposium during his trip and, on October 27, celebrated his 39th birthday. He recognized his alcoholism and knew plenty who shared his struggle. "An alcoholic is someone you don't like who drinks as much as you do," he purportedly observed.

On November 3, he felt unwell and stayed in bed drinking all day. He told his mistress and assistant, Liz Reitell, that he yearned to die and "go to the garden of Eden." That evening, he left the hotel for several hours, whereabouts unknown. He returned to his room and left again at 2 a.m. because he needed a drink. Off he went to the Horse.

Back at the Chelsea once more, he alleged that he'd had 18 whiskeys at the bar. "I think that's the record," he bragged to Reitell. That number, later disputed, was probably closer to six. The next day, he and Reitell went to the tavern for two beers. Still sick, Thomas decided to go back to the hotel. Reitell contacted the doctor who had given him injections a few weeks earlier to "revive" him before a performance of *Under Milk Wood*. The doctor arrived and injected him with morphine, which worsened Thomas's already labored breathing. By midnight, his face turned blue, prompting Reitell to call an ambulance, which transported him to St. Vincent's Hospital, mere blocks from the Horse. He fell into a coma, never regained consciousness, and died November 9. An autopsy attributed his death primarily to pneumonia, with brain swelling and a fatty liver as contributing factors.

The Horse was not without a poet in residence for too long. Another regular, Delmore Schwartz, took up the reins. He recited poetry, his own and others, to friends at the bar.

Two years after Thomas's death, Norman Mailer held court on Sunday afternoons. Mailer realized that the bar was a better place for entertaining friends than his East Village apartment because he wouldn't have trouble with guests who overstayed their welcome. Among those who joined Mailer, talking passionately about politics and literature, were Lawrence Ferlinghetti, John Clellon Holmes, and Herman Wouk.

Michael Harrington writes in his memoir that he went to the Horse every night for more than ten years: "As the people of Konigsberg were said to set their clocks by Immanuel Kant's walks, you would see me, punctually dissolute, appear on weeknights at midnight and on weekends at 1 o'clock." Jack Kerouac drank here once in a while. Someone wrote "KEROUAC GO HOME" above a urinal. James Baldwin, Jane Jacobs, Pete Hamill, Frank McCourt, Anaïs Nin, and Marguerite Young have all soaked in the Horse's atmosphere and booze, too.

After Thomas told audiences of his fondness for the Horse, "every English major in the Northeast Corridor began to make a pilgrimage to the White Horse," Harrington observed in 1972. Today, literature worshipers can wander the Dylan Thomas room to study the pictures of him, of his grave, and of his writing shed in Wales, alongside framed covers of his books. A plaque dedicating the room in 1986 quotes Thomas: "I like very much people telling me about their childhood, but they'll have to be quiet or else I'll be telling them about mine." Another plaque marks his table, which sits underneath a window.

The Horse itself is a historic relic, with its ornate hand-carved ceiling and worn oak floor. The solid mahogany bar, the original one, features brass railings and marks made over many decades. White horses, captured in ink, wood and ceramic, are tucked in here and there.

Order a drink, but be careful. The bartender may challenge you to 18 whiskeys.

Chumley's

86 Bedford Street (between Barrow and Grove streets)
chumleysnewyork.com
646-895-9813
Sunday through Thursday: 5:30 to 10:30 p.m.
Friday and Saturday: 5:30 to 11 p.m.

———————

The collapse of a chimney and a wall in 2007 nearly "eighty-sixed" Chumley's for good. Legend has it that the saying "to eighty-six" someone, meaning to eject them, originated at this former speakeasy, which opened in 1928 during Prohibition. Disorderly patrons were tossed out the back door, marked 86, the speakeasy's address. Linguists have not confirmed that bit of boozy lore.

After nine years of repairing it and its adjoining buildings and dealing with the staunch opposition of Village residents who feared its reopening would mark the return of raucous crowds, the new Chumley's was unveiled in 2016. *The WPA Guide to New York City* in the 1930s called it the "resort of the literati." Today, the owners call it the "preeminent American Writer's Bar," paying homage to its rich history.

Leland Stanford Chumley, who had been a stagecoach driver, soldier of fortune, freelance covered wagon driver, laborer, newspaper cartoonist, editorial writer, and a speakeasy waiter elsewhere, had taken the second floor of 86 Bedford for his publication, *The Radical*

Worker, in 1926. He was a Wobbly, that is, a member of the Industrial Workers of the World. In 1919, when the police were rounding up dangerous radicals, his publication's office was raided. Chumley was charged with carrying a large knife. "Don't let them kid you. I had a pocket knife," he told reporters.

Two years later, the social activist, who was often seen around the Village wearing a distinctive floppy hat and a wavy necktie, started his own speakeasy on the first floor of a former blacksmith's shop and stable on unassuming Bedford Street. He adapted the blacksmith's forge for use as a fireplace. No sign marked the entrance or back door. To get in, you needed to know the secret password.

In case the police were hankering to arrest more radicals or federal agents planned to target liquor law violators, Chumley had an escape plan: He installed a dumbwaiter that could ferry people to the second floor. A pre-existing tunnel with a trapdoor on the floor allowed alleged miscreants to wend their way to another house. Others could vacate the premises through the 86 Bedford Street exit while the cops came through the Pamela Court entrance.

Writers, including John Dos Passos, Theodore Dreiser, Upton Sinclair, and Floyd Dell, flocked to the speakeasy, which also served lunch and dinner. When their books were published, Chumley tacked the dust jackets to the walls. In 1935, two years after the end of Prohibition, Chumley died of a heart attack.

Much to the surprise of many, his widow, Henrietta, kept the place running. In between attending to the restaurant's operations, she sat at a table near the fireplace playing solitaire and swigging Manhattans until closing time, when a waiter nudged her awake. In his book *Greenwich Village and How It Got That Way*, Terry Miller writes that Henrietta died unnoticed at her table one evening in 1960. Everyone thought she had passed out, as was the case most nights. Her obituary simply states that she died at St. Vincent's Hospital.

Since her death, several owners have taken Chumley's under their wings. A bartender who went there for a nightcap in the sixties described it to a reporter as "a great memorable hangout never to be forgotten by those who loved lonely seedy bars where solitary men with notebooks seemed always huddled in a corner writing."

Over the years, numerous rumors, all untrue, were repeated about the authors who patronized the place. James Joyce did not write portions of *Ulysses* in a corner. Fact: Because of poor eyesight, he wrote it in red crayon while living in Zurich and Austria, and his novel was published before Chumley's opened. F. Scott Fitzgerald and Zelda Sayre did not have sex in a booth. And Ernest Hemingway did not need to take a lie-down on the second floor until he sobered up.

French writer Simone de Beauvoir did, however, become a regular in 1947. In her diary, published in book form as *America Day by Day* in 1948, she writes: "In Bedford Street is the only place in New York where you can read and work through the day, and talk through the night, without arousing curiosity or criticism: Chamby's [*sic*]." In another entry, "The room is square and utterly simple, with its little tables against the walls, but it has something so rare in America—atmosphere."

The cast of writers who toiled at their writing there by day or sought out Chumley's for a favorite cocktail and a meal is lengthy. Consider if all had been there at once. That would be the dream answer to the question, "What authors—dead or living—would you like to meet over a drink?" To name a few:

James Agee	W. Somerset Maugham
Djuna Barnes	Mary McCarthy
Brendan Behan	Frank McCourt
John Berryman	Jay McInerney
Maxwell Bodenheim	Margaret Mead
William S. Burroughs	Edna St. Vincent Millay
Willa Cather	Arthur Miller
John Cheever	Marianne Moore
Gregory Corso	Anaïs Nin
E. E. Cummings	Eugene O'Neill
Simone de Beauvoir	Henry Roth
William Faulkner	J. D. Salinger
Edna Ferber	Delmore Schwartz
Lawrence Ferlinghetti	Upton Sinclair
Allen Ginsberg	John Steinbeck
Erica Jong	William Styron
Alfred Kazin	Dylan Thomas
John F. Kennedy	Lowell Thomas
Jack Kerouac	James Thurber
Ring Lardner Jr.	Calvin Trillin
Sinclair Lewis	Thornton Wilder
Norman Mailer	Edmund Wilson

Notice that James Joyce is absent from this list. He never set foot in the United States.

By the time of the wall collapse, Chumley's had become, to put it nicely, a dive, a place where college students and off-duty firefighters from nearby Engine 24 went to quaff a few beers. One of the owners,

The nondescript door belies the inviting interior.

former fireman Jim Miller, enlisted a noted New York restaurateur to help him rescue the restaurant. The renovated Chumley's captures 1920s glamour, as interpreted by its new owner, Alessandro Borgognone. "It was important to me to bring back a piece of Greenwich Village history," he says. "I am excited to be a part of it and for the memories of Chumley's to live on."

The fireplace has been restored but cannot be used because of building codes. Over the fireplace hangs an original sketch of Leland Chumley by Joe Hill, a fellow Wobbly. While the interior has a smaller footprint than the original Chumley's did, the nineteenth-century facade, including the famed heavy door with its peephole, remain untouched (save for a good paint job) because it is a historical landmark. For the same reason, no sign will mark its existence. A writer of a 1930 guide to New York dining provides the street address, adding "From here on you'll have to work it out all by yourself, or ask a policeman, who probably won't be able to help you much either." He recommends calling the place to get directions from where you are. Luckily, this is the twenty-first century, when you can follow the dot on your smartphone's map app.

Readers and authors alike will be pleased to know that some 220 author photos and all the book jackets were salvaged during repairs; the unsalvageable ones were reprinted. They are mounted on the walls along the periphery of the restaurant and bar, like a literary shrine. Joe Gould, smoking a cigarette, looking mischievous. The portrait of O'Neill with his oh-so-serious face. Dust covers of the original editions of books by Dos Passos, Dreiser, Fitzgerald, Faulkner, Ginsberg, Moore, William Saroyan, Salinger, and Robert Lowell that make you want to dash off to a bookstore to savor their words. No need to rush, though, because the owners have more than six decades remaining on the lease.

CHAPLIN

Recipe courtesy of Chumley's

Chumley's mixologist looked to cocktail history and added a dash of whimsy when naming her drinks. Think old times and bootlegging meets *Mad Men*. When the characters played by Charlie Chaplin would get tipsy in his films, high jinks usually ensued. In his 1917 film, *The Adventurer*, Chaplin makes himself a strong cocktail: he sprays soda water into a bottle of whiskey and drinks it, only to spill it later. In the party scenes, after stealing a party guest's cocktail, he pours all the leftover cocktails into one glass for his own consumption.

INGREDIENTS

2 ounces blended scotch (or one with a deeper, smoky flavor profile)
¼ ounce Contratto Fernet
Bar spoon of maple syrup
Infused chocolate ice*
Orange peel (no white pith)

DIRECTIONS

Stir Scotch, Fernet, and syrup in a mixing glass. Strain into rocks glass over chocolate ice cube. Squeeze orange peel over drink to extract oils. Garnish with orange peel.

*Simmer a quart of water with a ¼ cup of cocoa nibs for 5 minutes. Let cool. Add a drop of orange blossom water, 2 drops of coffee extract, and 2 drops of almond extract. Freeze using 2-inch by 2-inch large ice cube molds.

Café Loup

105 West 13th Street (cross street: 6th Avenue)
cafeloupnyc.com
212-255-4746
Monday: 12 to 3 p.m. and 5:30 to 11:30 p.m.
Tuesday through Friday: 12 to 3 p.m. and 5:30 p.m. to midnight
Saturday: 5:30 to midnight
Sunday: 12 to 3:30 p.m. and 5:30 to 11:30 p.m.

———————

A decade before he died, Anglo-American journalist and author Christopher Hitchens wrote a tribute to Café Loup for *The Spectator*. He was teaching part time at the nearby New School and, as of 2001, had been coming to this establishment for about 20 years. He continued to do so until his last years.

This French bistro, which opened in the eighties, featured all Hitchens expected from a bar and restaurant: mid-morning opening for an espresso and a newspaper and a late-night, after-theater crowd enjoying cocktails; a bartender who recognizes a faithful patron and has his drink ready by the time he reaches the bar; music, no television; and some familiar faces. And if he wanted to "read, or write, or brood, or recuperate," Hitchens could do so here without interruption. He always ordered oysters followed by tarragon chicken, which remain on the menu. His spirit of choice? Whiskey on the rocks.

Café Loup attracts the denizens of the old Lion's Head, too. Editors and agents like to drop by the place and talk book deals. Literary journals throw book parties there. Writers, critics, and publishers converge here for the after-party the night the National Book Critics Circle awards its annual prizes. Paul Auster and Susan Sontag were once regulars. An author such as Mary Gaitskill might suggest meeting a reporter over lunch for an interview.

In 2014, when the cultural counselor of the French Embassy presented the insignia of the Order of Arts and Letters to Lorin Stein, the editor in chief of *The Paris Review*, he thanked Stein for introducing him to Café Loup. In the column "Ask *The Paris Review*," Stein wrote, "if you're in the Village and want to drink in the company of writers, you can't go wrong with Café Loup. It's crawling with them—and there's always plenty of extra martini in the shaker. If you're hungry, order the fries."

Gay Talese ranks it high on his list for the way his drink arrives. In 2012, he explained to *The Wall Street Journal*, "I like this downtown French bistro because it serves martinis at the table in the shaker. You thus get full measure, and the waiter doesn't spill drops of valuable gin on the floor while walking it to you."

Café Loup is a central hangout for students and faculty in The New School's creative writing program. In the early nineties Alexander Chee taught fiction writing in the program. He drank many Manhattans, his preferred cocktail, here. "Café Loup is an important place to me," he says.

Hitchens lamented that the bar, which dominates the room, could be a "fraction longer," though is nevertheless handsome. It still is. Pull up a barstool, and the veteran bartender may give you a taste of his current favorite wine, talk about the book he just finished reading, or mention that John Waters dropped in the other night. Black-and-white photos by

Berenice Abbott, Brassaï, and Irving Penn, mounted in black frames on the simple white walls with pieces of architectural fragments, add a quiet elegance. It feels like a bar and dining room set in an art gallery.

On Sunday nights, stop in for live jazz, an icy martini, and some bookish conversation.

MANHATTAN

At home, Alexander Chee and his partner drink perfect Manhattans, a smooth classic with muddy origins.

If you believe everything a bartender tells you, William F. Mulhall claimed in an 1823 essay that "the Manhattan cocktail was invented by a man named Black, who kept a place ten doors below Houston Street on Broadway in the [1860s]." In his era, Mulhall was a superstar bartender at the famed Hoffman House. In this century, cocktail historian David Wondrich did some sleuthing. Looking through city records, he uncovered a saloon owned by a William Black on Bowery Street above Houston Street in the 1870s. Mulhall's error on the location of Black's saloon casts doubt on the rest of his story.

There is also a theory that the Manhattan was created at the Manhattan Club in 1874, but that appears to be impossible. The story goes that the Manhattan was devised for a banquet held by Lady Randolph Churchill in honor of Samuel Tilden's election as governor of New York. The election was held November 3, 1874. Churchill gave birth to a son, Winston, on November 30 in England. Historians question whether the banquet occurred.

Historians do agree that a bartender did mix up the first Manhattan in the late 1800s somewhere in Manhattan, perhaps at the Manhattan Club.

INGREDIENTS

2 ounces rye or bourbon

½ ounce sweet vermouth

½ ounce dry vermouth

1 to 2 dashes Angostura bitters

Lemon peel

DIRECTIONS

Add all liquid ingredients to a cocktail shaker filled with ice. Strain into a chilled cocktail glass. Add lemon peel.

The Odeon

145 W. Broadway
theodeonrestaurant.com
212-233-0507
Monday through Friday: 8 to 11 a.m. (breakfast), 11 a.m. to 3 p.m.
(lunch), 3 to 5:30 p.m. (brasserie)
Dinner: Sunday and Monday: 5:30 to 10 p.m., Tuesday and Wednesday: 5:30 to 11 p.m.,
Thursday through Saturday: 5:30 p.m. to 12 a.m.
Saturday and Sunday: 10 a.m. to 4 p.m. (brunch); 4 to 5:30 p.m. (brasserie)

The Odeon is located in a section of lower Manhattan called Tribeca, which is south of Greenwich Village. In the early nineteenth century, long before the area was called Tribeca, writers James Fenimore Cooper and William Cullen Bryant lived here. Cooper had moved to the city to be closer to his publishers. He was living on the edge, so to speak, as Manhattanites had yet to crowd the rest of the island. To the north was the countryside, with farms and estates. In 1820, Cooper founded the Bread and Cheese Club, a group of New York City writers, editors, artists, and intellectuals. They saw their work as a bona fide vocation, not something they dabbled in. They met every two weeks for lunch and literary conversation. Cooper wanted the group to foster the young country's creative cred.

After decades as a commercial area, the "Triangle Below Canal," or TriBeCa, now a historic district, attracted creative types to cheap, roomy lofts in abandoned warehouse and factory buildings in the 1960s and 1970s. Since then, several buildings, including some Art Deco treasures, have been designated historic landmarks. These days, this approximately 40-block area has become a pricey, chic place to live that numerous celebrities call home. Due to its artsy roots, many cultural organizations—the eponymous film festival, for one—have settled here.

If the exterior of the Odeon looks familiar, that's because you have probably seen it on the cover of Jay McInerney's first novel, *Bright Lights, Big City*, published in 1984, and again on the cover of the third volume of what became a trilogy, *Bright, Precious Days*, published 32 years later. The first cover shows the Odeon in the shadow of the World Trade Center, which stood mere blocks south on the same street; the latest novel cover shows the art installation "Tribute in Light," which formed two vertical columns of light where the Twin Towers stood. (For a while, the Odeon was among the nightspots included in the opening montage of *Saturday Night Live*.) The Odeon hasn't changed much since McInerney set loose his debut oeuvre.

When this American-French bistro opened in 1980, Tribeca had none of the cachet it has today. By day, industrial activity enlivened the streets. At night, the cobblestone streets and cast-iron buildings around the Odeon looked like a noir-ish setting for a crime novel, devoid of cars and people, the gritty area an urban no-man's land. Cab drivers weren't keen on dropping off or picking up passengers. When a *New York Times* restaurant critic awarded it two out of four stars two months after opening, the Odeon became a destination. (Five blocks to its north is Beach Street, where James Fenimore Cooper once lived.)

Until the wee hours, the bar and restaurant were filled with writers, celebrities (Madonna, Cher, De Niro, the cast of *Saturday Night Live*), punk rockers (the Ramones), and artists (Basquiat, Warhol, Haring).

Denim and tuxedoes, Doc Martens and stilettos, all got along in this hot spot. Nights there could get out of hand in the cocaine-fueled eighties. Gossip columnists filled tabloids with tidbits of the patrons' debauchery.

McInerney, then a fact checker at *The New Yorker*, considered it an "oasis," setting a few scenes in his novels here. His first book party was held at the Odeon, of course, as was the one for its 20th anniversary edition. Other writerly types on the scene included Grove Atlantic president and publisher Morgan Entrekin, Christopher Hitchens, Carl Bernstein, Dirk Wittenborn, and Tom Wolfe in his bespoke white suits. Back then, the Odeon's last call was 4 a.m., after which everyone would crawl back to their lofts and tenements or uptown co-op apartments.

Nowadays, in a much busier Tribeca—day and night—the restaurant's red neon sign still exudes a warm retro vibe. That's no accident. The owners had to match the new sign to the original neon one, which spells out CAFETERIA on the side of the restaurant. The sign, a protected landmark, belonged to the Odeon's predecessor, a 1930s Art Deco diner called Tower Cafeteria that occupied the same address. The building dates back to 1869.

Entering the Odeon is like walking into a preserved time capsule. Decades after its opening, it feels as if it has been there forever. The interior has the original Art Deco walls, columns, and terrazzo floor that were part of the cafeteria. The chrome doors that lead to the kitchen have vintage yellow porthole windows. The spacious and airy room is lit by rippled glass sconces and round opaque pendant fixtures. The view of the entire establishment is unhindered from one end to the other, save for the columns here and there. Mirrors make the place seem bigger, its high ceilings still higher. Diners may sit in classic woven French bistro chairs or vintage red banquettes and booths. Patrons in search of reading

material to go with their drinks may grab a magazine from the rack that is attached to a column.

The mahogany bar, which takes up one wall, is the focal point of the room. The caramel-stained wood bar features rectilinear lines that end in smooth curves typical of Art Deco furniture. The owners sunk one-tenth of their opening budget into that beauty. The line of stainless steel cocktail shakers along the burnished bar seems more like a decorative Machine Age display than a set-up designed for the bartender's convenience. The shakers pick up the light and the chrome touches throughout the Odeon.

"The glittering, curvilinear surfaces inside Odeon are reassuring. The place makes you feel reasonable at any hour, often against bad odds, with its good light and clean luncheonette-via-Cartier deco décor," observes McInerney's aspiring writer-narrator in *Bright Lights, Big City*.

Much had changed by the 2000s, including McInerney's characters. Tribeca now has a Starbucks, a J. Crew, and parents with strollers on

steroids that seem more appropriate for extreme mountain hikes than city streets. The industrial warehouses have been renovated into condominiums that sell for millions of dollars. Catering to another era and a new scene, the restaurant closes no later than midnight and now opens for breakfast. Now that Condé Nast has relocated its headquarters from Times Square to One World Trade Center, you might glimpse, say, a *New Yorker* writer sipping a cocktail or *Vogue* editors in designer shoes having a power lunch.

THE COSMOPOLITAN

Recipe courtesy of the Odeon

The Cosmo is thought to have originated at the Odeon, although its current owners and staff aren't sure. Other sources say the Cosmo was invented here in 1988 by a bartender named Toby Cecchini.

INGREDIENTS

2 ounces citron vodka

¾ ounce Cointreau liquor

½ ounce fresh lime juice

½ ounce cranberry juice

Lime wedge

DIRECTIONS

Place all ingredients in an ice-filled shaker. Shake. Strain into a martini glass. Garnish with lime wedge.

GINGER MARTINI

Recipe courtesy of the Odeon

If the Cosmo seems so eighties, the Odeon has concocted its modern cousin, the bar's best-seller since around 2011. Fresh ginger kicks it up a notch.

INGREDIENTS

3 pieces of fresh ginger

2 ounces citron vodka

¾ ounce Cointreau

½ ounce fresh lemon juice

½ ounce simple syrup

¼ ounce fresh orange juice

DIRECTIONS

Muddle ginger in a cocktail shaker. Fill with ice. Add the remaining ingredients. Shake. Strain into martini glass.

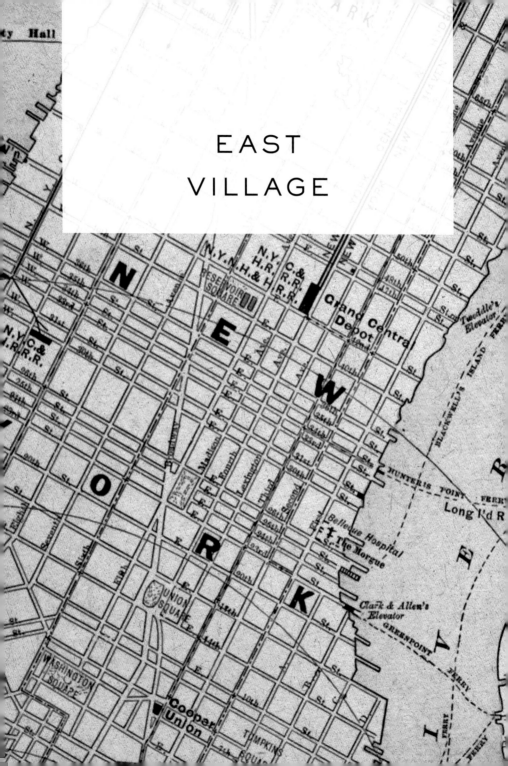

EAST
VILLAGE

The birthplace of the Nuyorican literary movement and home to Allen Ginsberg, William S. Burroughs, Sam Shepard, and W. H. Auden, the East Village is defined by Broadway to the west, the East River to the east (obviously), 14th Street to the north, and E. 1st Street to the south. This Manhattan neighborhood has undergone many makeovers. Originally, the area was considered part of the Lower East Side with its waves of immigrant settlers. In the 1950s, the neighborhood became the Beatniks' favorite place to hang their berets. Sometime in the early sixties, "East Village" first came into use along with the "incursion of hippies and flower children," according to the *American Institute of Architects Guide to New York City*.

In 1966, when reading series at coffeehouses and bars popular in the fifties and early sixties were on the wane, the Poetry Project was founded at St. Mark's Church-In-The Bowery. (One such East Village venue, the Five Spot Café, became the happening place for Beat poets who read their works, abstract expressionists who paid their bar tabs with their paintings, and legendary jazz musicians who performed at the club.) St. Mark's has hosted literary talks and readings since 1919, when Edna St. Vincent Millay, Kahlil Gibran, and Vachel Lindsay formed its arts committee. In 1926, William Carlos Williams gave a lecture as part of the church's Sunday Symposium series.

The Poetry Project, which continues to this day, has hosted a constellation of writers, including Miguel Algarín, Amiri Baraka, Allen Ginsberg, Gregory Corso, Jack Kerouac, Denise Levertov, Robert Lowell, Jayne Anne Phillips, Ishmael Reed, Saint Geraud (a.k.a. Bill Knott), and Patti Smith.

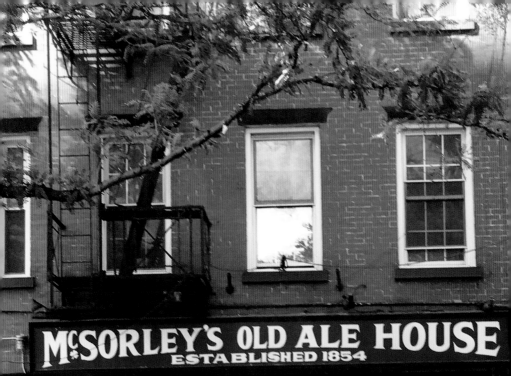

McSorley's Old Ale House

15 E. 7th Street (between 2nd and 3rd avenues)
mcsorleysoldalehouse.nyc
212-473-9148
Monday through Saturday: 11 a.m. to 1 a.m.
Sunday: 1 p.m. to 1 a.m.

———————

Among the bohemians who quaffed ale here was E. E. Cummings. In one of his collections of poetry, published in 1923, a poem beginning "i was sitting in mcsorley's" notes the beauty of the falling snow, while inside it is "snug and evil." This ne plus ultra dive bar with its sawdust-covered floors was later profiled by Joseph Mitchell for *The New Yorker* in 1940. The saloon, which has served only light and dark mugs of its own ale except for a brief stint serving liquor, since its arrival on New York's saloon scene, has become a literary mecca.

The museum-like landmark's origin on this site dates to 1854, the year John McSorley claims he opened his bar, then known as This Old House at Home. However, a 2012 NYC Landmarks Preservation Commission Report details some discrepancies in records for the lot.

City tax records show the lot was vacant until 1860 or 1861. Yet the value of the property increased between 1848 and 1856, an indication that a small structure most likely existed, although not recorded. That small structure may have housed the bar and generated enough rent for the owner to cover property taxes. By 1861, the owner had built a two-story building, according to tax records for that year.

The Italianate-style building that houses McSorley's today was built circa 1865. The crowded tenements nearby brought him a steady stream of thirsty laborers, workers, and the unemployed. In 1908, a storm knocked the original sign down. With a new sign, McSorley, a native of Ireland, put his family's name on the bar. During Prohibition, the saloon continued serving its customers, including members of the Tammany Hall political machine, policemen, and federal agents, without the threat of raids, fines, or closure.

After McSorley's death in 1910, his son took over. "His one pious passion is to maintain the spirit of the place and the spirit of his father," Hutchins Hapgood wrote in a 1913 profile of the bar for *Harper's Weekly*. An illustration accompanying the story prompted Christopher Morley, a journalist and an author, to check out the watering hole. He discovered it to be "a fine-old Tammany-flavoured [*sic*] sanctum" with a "genteel air of literature and politics and sentiment that belongs to an honest saloon." Morley considered it the "last toll-gate on the Bohemian frontier." During Prohibition, Morley would sit at a table beneath the Robert Burns por-trait or by the window with a pad of paper and sharpened pencil. "Would there be any more propitious place in New York at which to fashion verses?" he wrote.

There is no doubt that sawdust from the ale house's early years lingers today in some corner. The sawdust was spread on the floor to catch whatever the spittoons didn't, plus any beer spills. Today, shuffling through the occasional mound of sawdust is like traipsing through a cat's litter box.

Spittoons have fallen out of favor, but decades of bric-a-brac and photographs have accumulated on the walls and in every nook and cranny, some of which Abraham Lincoln may have looked over when the parched soon-to-be president stopped in after giving a speech. Crane your neck in every direction and you'll spot shackles belonging to a Civil War POW, campaign buttons, numerous police badges, and a pair of handcuffs behind the bar.

Search for Berenice Abbott's photos, newspaper clippings that date back to Abraham Lincoln's assassination, the original "Wanted" poster for John Wilkes Boothe, and a framed book jacket of Joseph Mitchell's *McSorley's Wonderful Saloon*. A signed photo of Socks, the Clintons' cat when Bill was president, hangs in the back room: "To Minnie, with best wishes, Love Socks 2-19-94." Minnie was one of a long line of felines that were denizens of the bar until the city health department scotched that. Any bare dark wood is scratched with patrons' initials and indecipherable whatnot. Behind

Your two beer choices—light or dark—come in a pair of mugs.

the bar, the original beer dispenser—its "glush of squirting taps" that Cummings celebrated now mute—and icebox serve as landing places for more knick-knacks, antique shotguns, and old ceramic steins.

One curiosity hangs from the ceiling: turkey wishbones dangling on the old gas lamp. These may have been left by doughboys hoping to retrieve them after surviving the war, or else McSorley liked his wishbones. In 2011, the city health department inspectors intimated that the bones needed to be relieved of their deep strata of cobwebs and dust.

This old beer spigot is one of many original features.

Had the dust and the bones been carbon-dated, it might have revealed particles of World War I–era pedigree. The proprietor, Matthew Maher, gathered the dust in a box and took it home for safekeeping. Absent the dust, patrons can discern the bones' true shapes.

The bar's tagline was "Good Ale, Raw Onions, and No Ladies" until 1970, when the bar lost a discrimination lawsuit. The newspaper, commemorating the first women served at the bar, headlined "14 High Heels Stir Sawdust at McSorley's," is up there on a wall, of course.

Lean on the beaten, scratched wooden bar (no stools) with a foot on the brass rest. It accommodates "ten elbows," Mitchell writes. Sit at a round table so worn that the brass hardware holding it together peeks through the wooden top. A server in a floor-length white apron will ask "light or dark?" Moments later, two small glass mugs sloshing with "the ale, which never lets you grow old," as Cummings writes, are delivered to the table. The reason for the two mugs instead of one larger one is a mystery.

Hungry patrons may order from a limited chalkboard menu. The cheese plate consists of those infamous raw onions, crackers, cheddar cheese, and McSorley's hot mustard. In winter, feel free to heat your mug on the potbellied stove in the front room. "Old John [McSorley] maintained that the man never lived who needed a stronger drink than a mug of stock ale warmed on the hob of a stove," Mitchell writes.

Above all, dawdle and eavesdrop. No music will interrupt your thoughts. Imagine the likes of Brendan Behan, Frank and Malachy McCourt, Hunter S. Thompson, and Amiri Baraka finding refuge here, as they were wont to do after a day plugging away at their typewriters, the fading yellow sunlight bathing the walls.

K GB Bar

The Red Room at KGB

85 E. 4th Street (near 2nd Avenue)
kgbbar.com
redroomnyc.com
347-441-4481
Daily: 7 p.m. to 4 a.m.

———————

Red metal doors at the entrance to this 1920s brick building lead to a set of uneven marble stairs, which lead in turn to a small, dimly-lit second-floor bar with high ceilings. The climb and the entrance create an air of intrigue, of state secrets. The color of the KGB bar's walls and curtains could be called Communist Red. Light bounces off the glossy red walls and ceiling, casting everything and everyone, even sober new arrivals, in a flushed glow. In this small space, writers ranging from venerated to unknown have been reading from their works to standing-room-only audiences since the mid-nineties.

Beginning in 1948, the building belonged to the Ukrainian Labor Home, a social club for expat Ukrainian socialists. During the McCarthy era, any signs of their socialist leanings were hidden. The first floor was reserved for parties and banquets. Upstairs was their private bar. When he was a kid, Denis Woychuk drank there with his Ukrainian dad and his cronies from the old country. The 5-year-old Woychuk was given small shots of vodka and whiskey. In the 1980s, he studied law, but the arts had his heart. Meanwhile, the declining club needed money to stay viable. The aging Ukrainians turned to Woychuk. He opened the Kraine Gallery for art exhibitions and later theater performances on the first floor. The elderly Ukrainian socialists continued their covert drinking upstairs.

The gallery didn't survive the 1987 stock market crash, but the performance space was profitable. Woychuk, by then a practicing lawyer and a writer without any experience operating a bar decided to open one on the second floor. Given its history, he wanted to name it the KGB Bar, but the state governmental agency wouldn't let him register a corporation named after the KGB, the Soviet Union's state security agency. He had another idea for a name. His new corporation would be named after the gallery: Kraine Gallery Bar. KGB. A small neon sign was suspended over the door. He decorated its walls with authentic Soviet–era propaganda posters and photos of famous Soviets, such as the first woman cosmonaut, Valentina Tereshkova, that he found secreted in the building. An old red USSR flag bearing the hammer and sickle hangs over the bar.

Meanwhile, the bar was not making ends meet. Woychuk hired Dan Christian, also a published writer, who had bar management chops. The two envisioned a place where writers could join them and talk shop. They could also read from their works and be comped with a few drinks. Despite the fact that admission to the readings would be free, customers were not expected to drink. In the summer of 1994, they held the bar's first reading. Junot Diaz, A. M. Homes, Elissa Schappell, and Rick Moody have all taken turns in front of the crowd. After a story in *The New York Times*, the bar and its reading series with celebrated and up-and-coming writers took off.

On Sunday evenings, come for your fiction fix. Return on Monday for the poetry. Tuesdays through Thursdays, other readings are held. The bar publishes an online journal, *KGB Bar Lit*. In 2002, they published *On the Rocks: The KGB Bar Fiction Anthology*, featuring provocative and bold works by such luminaries as Mary Gaitskill, Jonathan Lethem, Aimee Bender, Dani Shapiro, Joyce Carol Oates, and Francine Prose, alongside those who have toiled in obscurity.

Since 2002, the Liars League has held an event at KGB for new writers. On a summer night, four stories, one by a better known but still emerging writer, are read by actors. Attendees arrive carrying their subway reading: the latest issue of *Harper's Weekly*, a worn copy of a Faulkner novel. Within a half hour, the room is packed. At a lectern crammed into a corner stands the host of tonight's readings, his face lit by the tiny lamp like a kid under the blanket with a flashlight and a book. KGB Bar's shadowy, intimate space provides an atmosphere reminiscent of sitting around a campfire telling and listening to stories. Instead of crickets chirping and owls hooting, sirens occasionally take you out of the moment.

Woychuk opened an upscale speakeasy, The Red Room, tucked upstairs on the third floor in 2014. The building housed a real speakeasy/casino/brothel in 1922 called Palm Casino run by mobster Lucky Luciano. In addition to literary readings and NY Writers Workshops, The Red Room books musical guests. One ensemble that has performed upstairs is "The Corrections," featuring lead vocals by novelist Rebecca Donner and backed by James Wood, Harvard professor and literary critic for *The New Yorker*, plus a bassist, keyboardist, and saxophonist. The band's name is taken from the Jonathan Franzen novel, which Wood reviewed negatively.

At the KGB Bar, straight vodka is a top seller. The Red Room's cocktails evoke Prohibition and mobsters: Cocksman, Wiseguy, and Casino Cocktail, as well as classic 1920s cocktails.

MOSCOW MULE

Vodka, that tasteless, colorless, odorless Russian spirit made from fermented potatoes or grains, did not capture America's fancy until the 1940s and 1950s. *New Yorker* food and travel writer A. J. Liebling sniffed, "It is the ideal intoxicant for the drinker who wants no reminder of how hurt mother would be if she knew what he was doing."

Picture three businessmen who were friends at the end of their workday at the bar of the Chatham Hotel in New York in 1941. "We three were quaffing a slug, nibbling an hors d'oeuvre and shoving toward inventive genius," John G. Martin, president of G.F. Heublein Brothers, told a *New York Herald Tribune* reporter in 1948. The other two men were John Morgan, owner of the Cock'n Bull Restaurant in Hollywood, and Rudolph Kunett, president of Pierre Smirnoff, Heublein's vodka division. Morgan, whose side business was making ginger beer, had driven across the plains with a carload of ginger beer in crockery bottles.

"Ice was ordered, limes procured, mugs ushered in and the concoction was put together. Cups were raised, the men counted five and down went the first taste. It was good. It lifted the spirit to adventure," the *Herald Tribune* reporter writes. After downing four or five of their invention, the three christened it the Moscow Mule.

A different account says that the Moscow Mule originated not at the Chatham Hotel but at Morgan's Hollywood restaurant. Martin was having difficulty establishing a market for his vodka in California. Morgan was stuck with plenty of jugs of his ginger beer because that too proved a difficult sell. They had a lightbulb moment and mixed the first Moscow Mule. The third person in this version is Morgan's girlfriend, who had copper mugs she needed to unload. In 1942, a newspaper columnist writes of a new drink, the Moscow Mule, "that is a craze in the movie colony now."

Wherever the truth lies, that tasteless vodka now had its own cocktail. With the resurgence of cocktails, those shiny copper mugs can be spotted at bars and *nouveau* speakeasies everywhere.

INGREDIENTS

2 ounces vodka

1 ounce fresh lime juice

Ginger beer

1 lime wedge

DIRECTIONS

In a highball glass or copper mug filled with ice, add vodka and lime juice. Top with ginger beer. Stir with a stirring rod or chopstick. Garnish with lime.

Nuyorican Poets Cafe

236 E. 3rd Street (between Avenue A and Avenue B)
nuyorican.org
212-780-9386
See events calendar for hours

The Nuyorican Poets Cafe grew out of a regular gathering of poets in the living room of Miguel Algarín, a Puerto Rican poet and literature professor at Rutgers University, in 1973. Nuyorican, a portmanteau of New York and Puerto Rican, refers to the island residents who settled in the city. In 1981, and several venues later as its audience grew and grew, they bought the tenement it now occupies.

Early performers included Algarín, William S. Burroughs, Gregory Corso, Allen Ginsberg, Amiri Baraka, Lucky Cienfuegos, Pedro Pietro, and Miguel Piñero. Ginsberg and his Beats entourage, consisting of Corso and Burroughs, stumbled on the Nuyo by chance in the seventies. Algarín was sweeping up at one of their interim locales when Ginsberg poked his head in. He asked what was going on. "I smell a scene," he said to Algarín. At that night's reading, the crowd booed Burroughs off the stage. Ginsberg deemed it "the most integrated place on the planet."

The Nuyo lays claim to holding New York City's first poetry slam in 1989. This nonprofit cultural institution has since become woven into the city's cultural DNA. While not a bar per se, the cafe has a bartender who serves alcoholic and nonalcoholic refreshments during its famous poetry slams. The Nuyo opens for performances only.

At the Friday night slams, poets of all levels, ages, and ethnicities may participate. The judges are chosen at random from an audience that may number as high as 300. Anyone nostalgic for the edginess of the Beats' readings should attend. The Nuyo also holds open-mic nights, prose and poetry readings, theater performances, visual art exhibitions, and hip-hop and Latin jazz concerts.

In 2018, the building will be gutted, and storage rooms will be transformed into additional performance and classroom spaces. During the yearlong renovation, the organization will hold its events at various locations.

Its anthology, *Aloud: Voices from the Nuyorican Poets Cafe*, published in 1994 and recipient of an American Book Award, provides a taste of its performances.

PLUM DAIQUIRI

On one of his visits to San Juan, Puerto Rico, his mother's native city, William Carlos Williams—Allen Ginsberg's mentor—had the best daiquiris he'd ever tasted. In his autobiography, he doesn't mention the cocktail's ingredients, but one can safely bet that rum from one of the island's distilleries was in the mix. This daiquiri pays homage to Williams' poem, "This is just to say." After taking a plum from the icebox, don't forget to leave a note.

INGREDIENTS

1 fresh plum, quartered, peeled, stone removed
2 ounces Puerto Rican light rum
½ ounce fresh lime juice
½ ounce simple syrup
Mint leaf, lime wedge, or plum slice for garnish

DIRECTIONS

In a cocktail shaker, muddle the plum to release its juices. Add ice and the other ingredients. Shake vigorously. Using a fine strainer, pour into chilled martini glass. Add garnish.

Note: Increase amount of simple syrup if plums are not fully ripe.

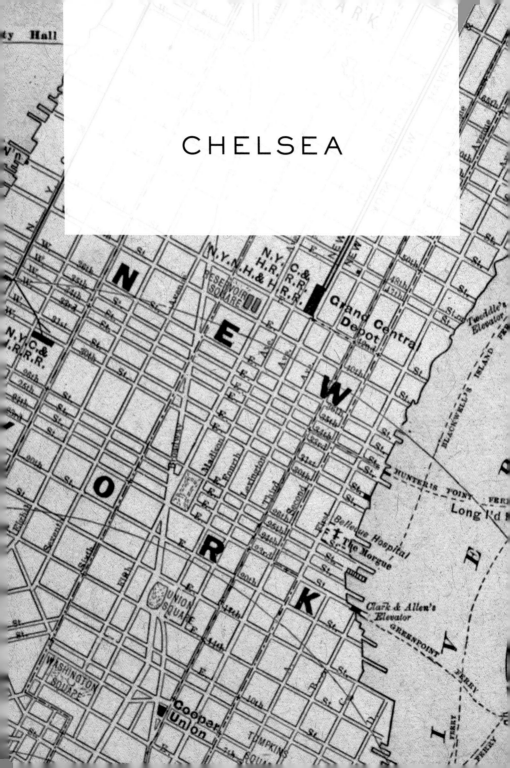

CHELSEA

A poet's grandfather unwittingly gave this thriving haven for artists its moniker when he named his estate "Chelsea" on what is now 21st Street in the latter half of the eighteenth century. The estate was surrounded by an apple orchard and countryside, two to three miles north of the then inhabited portion of New York. New Yorkers went berry picking in the vicinity of what is now W. 31st Street.

The author of "A Visit from St. Nicholas," Clement C. Moore, was born on the Chelsea estate in 1779 and inherited the property. In 1811, much to his consternation city planners determined Manhattan's street grid, with 9th Avenue going straight through the property. Moore went into the real estate business. He subdivided the estate into lots, sold them to affluent city dwellers, and made a nice sum of money as a result. In 1827, he donated a portion of his property to the Episcopal diocese for its seminary, which still stands today on 9th Avenue and 21st Street. Some of his parcels were underwater. In the 1850s, the city filled those, extending the width of Manhattan.

Mills, warehouses, factories, and railroad freight yards populated the waterfront, while wealthy people built row houses and homes farther east. In one brownstone, number 14 on Chelsea's main thoroughfare, W. 23rd Street, Edith Newbold Jones was born in 1862. We know her by her married name, Edith Wharton. The brownstone, which still stands, is marked by a dinner-plate-size red plaque commemorating its place in American literature and by a much larger green Starbucks sign.

In the late 1800s, Manhattan's theater district relocated to W. 23rd Street. With the advent of motion pictures, cinema companies moved into spacious buildings in the industrial section. In 1977, Chelsea, bounded by 14th and 34th streets (some say 30th), as well as 6th Avenue and the Hudson River, was listed on the U.S. National Register of Historic Places. By the late 1990s, galleries and artists of all types were populating this largely residential area. With the 1997 opening of the Chelsea Market in the former National Biscuit Company plant, where the Oreo was invented, and the 2009 unveiling of the High Line, on old elevated railroad tracks, Chelsea continues its evolution.

Hotel Chelsea/El Quijote Restaurant

222 W. 23rd Street (between 7th and 8th avenues)
elquijoterestaurant.com
212-929-1855
Sunday through Thursday: 11:30 a.m. to midnight
Friday and Saturday: 11:30 a.m. to 1 a.m.

In her memoir, *Just Kids*, Patti Smith tells of the time she and Robert Mapplethorpe were living at the Chelsea in 1969 and frequenting El Quijote, named for the Cervantes novel. "It was a bar-restaurant adjacent to the hotel, connected to the lobby by its own door, which made it feel like our bar," she writes. She knew its history as the place where many literati "had raised one too many a glass." (In those days, Smith worked at the resplendent two-level Scribner's Bookstore, in a Beaux-Arts building on Fifth Avenue. A makeup chain store occupies the space now, but the interior of the bookstore remains.)

El Quijote, owned by Spanish Civil War refugees, served its first tapas and sangria in 1930. However, the hotel started out as an experiment in apartment living in 1884. Pioneering architect Philip Hubert, a Frenchman who settled in America, designed the monolithic 12-story building to look like Parisian architecture: slate roof, intricate iron balconies with sunflower ornaments, dormer windows, and a rooftop garden. The apartments consisted of three to ten rooms to suit a range of budgets. Hubert saw it as a place for the laborers who built it, musicians, artists, and writers. Artist studios occupied the top floor. The residents shared the costs of utilities and ate in one of three communal dining rooms. In 1891, novelist and former editor of *The Atlantic Monthly*, William Dean Howells moved in and complained in a letter to his father about his expensive abode.

By 1903, Hubert's experiment, New York's first co-op apartments, went bankrupt. Financial panics and the relocation of several theaters farther north contributed to its failure. In 1905, the apartments were subdivided, and the building was converted into a residential hotel, which also became insolvent. But its life as an ad hoc artists' colony took hold.

Over those many decades, the Chelsea had become an inspiring incubator for the Beats and other literary types. Chapter and verse, on paper and in real life, were written in its rooms, in its lobby, and in its restaurant. The tales were beautiful or tragic or both. Some were laced with a little bit of rock and roll, punk, and paint.

First, the Bohemians came. Mark Twain lived here for a bit shortly after it became a hotel. Twain, who discovered the delights of a whiskey cocktail while in London, dined with the Howellses there. "Sometimes too much to drink is barely enough," Twain once said. Another early resident, Edgar Lee Masters, wrote of it in his poem "The Hotel Chelsea." When his editors and creditors went after him, William Sydney Porter, whose pen name was O. Henry, took a room

under another assumed name. Thomas Wolfe signed in on the recommendation of Masters. A photo shows the towering 6-foot-6 Wolfe
in Room 829, his foot resting on a crate crammed with manuscripts,
including the one for *You Can't Go Home Again*. At the hotel bar, a
fellow writer, Ella Winter, told Wolfe, "Don't you know you can never
go home again?" Her comment lifted him out of his writer's block and
helped him understand the point of his mammoth novel, published
posthumously in 1940.

The Beats shuffled in during the fifties. Jack Kerouac tinkered on
his breakthrough novel, *On the Road*, while living there. After a night
of drinking, he and Gore Vidal had a one-night stand here (see Minetta
Tavern). Other Beats who were tenants include William S. Burroughs,
Allen Ginsberg, and Gregory Corso.

Arthur Miller visited Dylan Thomas in 1953 when Miller asked
him to join him on a discussion panel. Apparently, Thomas's shabby
room didn't put Miller off, who moved there and wrote his play *After
the Fall*. Thomas spent his final days in Room 205 before dying at St.
Vincent's Hospital.

During the sixties, the neighborhood and the hotel had become even
seedier. But that didn't stop scores of writers from hanging their shingle
there. A frequent guest, Arthur C. Clarke (Room 322) plugged away on
2001: A Space Odyssey while a resident. Miller returned here and called
it home for six years after his divorce from Marilyn Monroe in 1961.
"This hotel does not belong to America," Miller wrote. "There are no
vacuum cleaners, no rules and shame . . . it's the high spot of surreal.
Cautiously, I lifted my feet to move across bloodstained winos passing
out on the sidewalks—and I was happy. I witnessed how a new time, the
sixties, stumbled into the Chelsea with young, bloodshot eyes."

Brendan Behan joined the surreal scene in 1963, after the Algonquin tossed him out for his drunken antics. He resumed his drinking at El Quijote. Poet Leonard Cohen, who lived in several rooms, including Room 424 in the sixties, was moved to write two songs, "Chelsea Hotel #1" and "Chelsea Hotel #2." In 1969, Patti Smith (Room 1017) and Sam Shepard hung out together, reading. Pete Hamill, while living there in the nineties, wrote *Snow in August*. In his novel *Tabloid City*, one of the characters, an aging artist, resides in the Chelsea.

At a 1966 hearing, the New York City Board of Estimate was considering whether the hotel deserved landmark status. Several resident writers, including Charles Jackson, author of *The Lost Weekend*, attested to the hotel's fabled history. With his advance, he had moved there to work on another novel after years of substance abuse and writer's block. The local community planning board deemed it a "shabby institution" that was "unattractive and second rate." Indifferent to their objections, the Estimate Board declared that this distinguished hotel, home to numerous famous writers, was a landmark. Two years later, Jackson, at age 65, overdosed on sleeping pills in his room at the Chelsea.

The hotel was run by the same family for nearly 70 years, until the board booted out the son in 2007. In 2011, a real estate developer purchased it, only to be bought out by his partner in 2013. The Hotel Chelsea, with a few remaining tenants, awaits in limbo and is shrouded in scaffolding as of this writing. The numerous plaques listing its famous guests are nevertheless visible.

El Quijote, the hotel's only place to drink and dine since 1930, the place where Smith and her fellow Chelsea tenants feasted on tequila, paella, and sangria, was sold to the hotel's new owner in 2014. "The overall goal is to retain the signature look and feel of El Quijote while maintaining its authenticity and history, which are already woven into that of Hotel Chelsea," a spokesman told a reporter.

The ambience gets a boost from a trio of longtime New Yorkers, all natives of Spain, at the bar. Regulars, these three white-haired men gab and philosophize in Spanish over lunch. The waitstaff wear black Eton waist jackets with "El Quijote" embroidered on them, seemingly dressed for another era. A bulky vintage brass cash register is parked on the bar. The long wood bar, where James Salter met Robert Phelps, has infinite cigarette burns, the varnish along its edge worn from years of forearms leaning against it. Everywhere, sculptural and print representations of Don Quixote dress up shelves and walls. Ditto windmills, bulls, and toreadors. A large mural that looms over the dining room and bar depicts—wait for it—scenes from Cervantes's novel. At the time I was there, a man on a spiritual journey talking about Dylan Thomas sat at the bar a few stools down. Spanish flamenco music with its percussive guitars plays on the sound system.

ADDITIONAL WRITERS WHO CHECKED IN

Charles Bukowski

Jim Carroll

Quentin Crisp

Melvil Dewey (known for the Dewey Decimal System)

James T. Farrell

Isabella Gardner

Ethan Hawke

Vladimir Nabokov

Joseph O'Neill

James Schuyler

Wallace Shawn

Terry Southern

Piri Thomas

Virgil Thomson

Yevgeny Yevtushenko

GIN-TONIC

El Quijote's sangria recipe is a secret, but no problem. Instead, make the on-trend drink Spaniards are so *obsesionado* with: They've dispensed with the ampersand and the lime wedge and dressed it up. A sprig of a botanical, such as thyme, mint, lavender, basil, fennel, cilantro, or rosemary, complements similar flavors in the gin. Then add a few citrus peels, grapes, some berries, or a cucumber slice to round it off. For spice, consider star anise or a cinnamon stick. Try different combinations, but don't overload the glass. Bartenders serve the icy beverage in a large copa de balon, a balloon-shaped wine glass, which accentuates the aromas reaching your nose.

INGREDIENTS

2 ounces London dry gin

3 ounces tonic water (for a better flavor, avoid ones made with high fructose corn syrup
  or preservatives)

Large ice cubes

Sprig of a botanical, slapped between your hands to release the oils

Citrus peel with no pith (for added color, combine two different types)

Two or three berries or cucumber slices (optional)

DIRECTIONS

Place garnishes in the bottom of the glass. Pour gin over the garnishes. Fill the glass with as many ice cubes as will fit in the glass. Add tonic. (In Spain, bartenders pour the tonic over the back of a bar spoon into the glass.)

The Half King
Bar and Restaurant

505 W. 23rd Street
thehalfking.com
212-462-4300
Monday through Friday: 11 a.m. to 4 a.m.
Saturday and Sunday: 9 a.m. to 4 a.m.

War correspondents the world over have long had beloved bars they would retreat to after a day covering battles. While covering the Spanish Civil War in the thirties, Ernest Hemingway had several favorite haunts throughout Spain. Veteran war correspondent and author Sebastian Junger, who has witnessed combat and its tragedies firsthand in Afghanistan, Kosovo, and Liberia, yearned for such an outpost in his adopted home, New York City. The city, he felt, lacked a place where people in the publishing and film industries could meet and have a sense of community.

"People are social animals, and they like to gather. War reporters do it overseas on assignment—the infamous hotel bar," says Junger, author of the best-seller *A Perfect Storm*. "We thought we would just provide that in New York."

He, journalist Scott Anderson, and documentarian Nanette Burstein joked about owning a place that had a firehouse pole leading from their apartment into a downstairs bar in the Red Hook section of Brooklyn. They found a spot with two large rooms in a then marginal area of Manhattan with low rents. The Half King, named for a Native American chief during the French and Indian War, opened in 2000. In warm weather, patrons can enjoy the sidewalk cafe seating and a garden in back. Alas, there is no brass pole.

From the get-go, the owners envisioned a robust reading series. The first room consists of the bar, some booths, and tables. The second room feels like a family room, with couches, books, board games, and tables. Here is where the Half King's esteemed event takes place. Now a Chelsea institution, 50 to 60 literary events and photojournalism exhibitions are held in this room each year. Every Monday, published authors—no poets, however—read from new works, with magazine editors and writers regularly showcasing their work to packed audiences. The works chosen often have some controversial or political edge. Spirited discussions are encouraged.

Junger and his co-owners, however, didn't want their watering hole mistaken for a pretentious literary salon filled with ponderous sorts. The Half King's décor is made of reclaimed wood that came from salvage yards and a 200-year-old Mennonite barn in Pennsylvania—it's a bar with grit.

A lone photo hangs permanently on the barroom's far wall. It commemorates photojournalist Tim Hetherington, a friend and collaborator of Junger's. Hetherington died while covering the civil war in Libya. He was hit by shrapnel fired by Colonel Muammar Gaddafi's forces. The two co-directed the Oscar-nominated feature-length documentary *Restrepo*, which follows the deployment of U.S. soldiers to Afghanistan.

In the wake of Hetherington's death, Junger decided he no longer wanted to do war reporting. Instead, Junger launched a nonprofit organization called Reporters Instructed in Saving Colleagues (RISC). The organization holds three-day courses during which freelance war correspondents learn frontline combat medicine.

Literature lovers can nurse a tropical cocktail while reading war novels or reportage by Junger, Anderson, Hemingway, Margaret Fuller, Graham Greene, or Martha Gellhorn. When you order a drink, note the framed knife blade above the liquor bottles on the bar. When Anderson was on assignment for *The New York Times*, he visited an open-air penal colony on a Panamanian island. A prison guard offered him the crude shiv, made by an inmate.

WHISKEY CAIPIRINHA WITH MINT

Recipe courtesy of the Half King

This take on Brazil's national cocktail is served during the summer months at the Half King. The bartender substitutes whiskey for Brazil's cachaça, a rum-like spirit made from sugar cane. Brazilians are proud of their national product. But never call cachaça "Brazilian rum."

INGREDIENTS

8 mint leaves

1 teaspoon sugar

1 ounce fresh lemon juice

2 ounces honey-flavored whiskey

DIRECTIONS

In a large rocks glass, muddle mint leaves with sugar. Add lemon juice and honey whiskey. Pour into a shaker with ice and shake vigorously. Pour back into the large rocks glass. Garnish with a sprig of mint.

The Whiskey Caipirinha

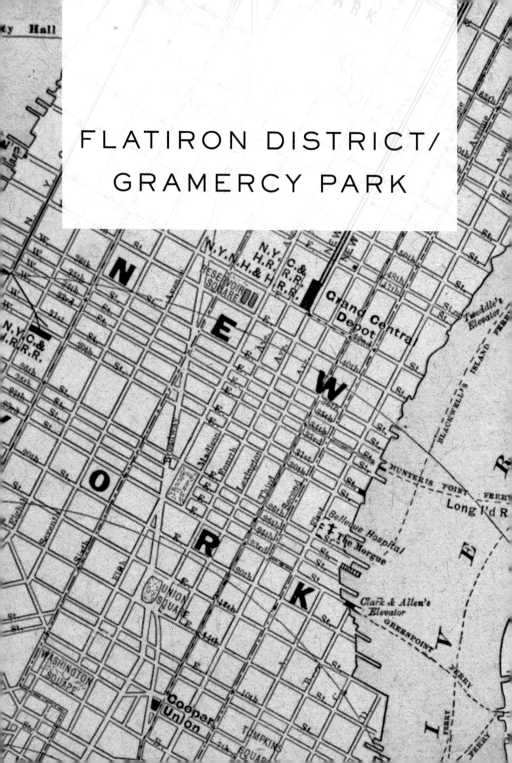

FLATIRON DISTRICT/ GRAMERCY PARK

The Flatiron District is the birthplace of Theodore Roosevelt, who was the author of 42 books in addition to being the 26th president of the United States. It is also the location of several publishers. Until 1914, this swath of Manhattan was known as the Ladies' Mile because of the posh fashion department stores found there. In the late twentieth century, the area became known as the Flatiron District because of the renowned wedge-shaped Flatiron Building in its midst. The building itself has hosted a variety of publishing industry tenants since it first opened.

The Gramercy Park area gets its name from the eponymous gated park, which is accessible only to residents of the surrounding apartments. Together, the boundaries of the area covered by Gramercy Park and the Flatiron District are defined by Chelsea to the west and Greenwich Village and the East Village to the south. Its northern edge is considered to be 34th Street from the East River to Broadway.

Famous literary residents include John Steinbeck, Hart Crane, Booth Tarkington, Oscar Wilde, O. Henry, and Herman Melville. Garth Williams's illustrations for E. B. White's *Stuart Little* show the Little family living at Four Gramercy Park. James Harper, the founder of Harper and Sons (now HarperCollins), lived in the same townhouse until he died in 1869. The book was published by Harper & Brothers in 1945.

OLD TOWN
BAR
RESTAURANT

Old Town Bar

45 E. 18th Street (between Broadway and Park Avenue South)
oldtownbar.com
212-529-1003
Monday through Friday: 11:30 a.m. to 11:30 p.m.
Saturday: 12 to 11:30 p.m.
Sunday: 12 to 10 p.m.

———

The first owner of Old Town started out as a copy boy for *The New York Sun*. Instead of working his way to the police beat and the journalist's most coveted assignment, columnist Larry Meagher left the newspaper business to open a few bars in Brooklyn, his home turf. In the 1970s, he shuttered his Brooklyn bars and hightailed it over to Manhattan, where he became manager of the Old Town Bar, which has been around since 1892. Meagher eventually bought the bar. His son, Gerard, is now a co-owner of this unpretentious, convivial watering hole.

"Brooklyn was where he made his mistakes," Gerard says. His father nailed it with Old Town. Absent are televisions and music. "We're about conversation," Gerard says. "Everybody is treated the same. We don't play up to celebrities." He takes pride, as his father did, in Old Town's lack of attitude and in the fact that it is not a hipster or singles bar. And the writers do come to quaff—or, as in one case, to imagine imbibing again.

Before we get to the highbrow literary stuff, this bar is renowned for one other reason: porcelain, specifically its urinals. The Hinsdale urinals, installed on November 1, 1910 (the date is etched on the top of each one), are about the size of an average bathtub standing on end. On the urinals' 100th anniversary, the owners held a bash, complete with a champagne toast, flowers, and balloons. The bar was chock-full for the celebration. Former *Sports Illustrated* columnist and author Steve Rushin regaled them with a tribute. He has written that these urinals are "the greatest achievements in porcelain since Belleek made its first tea set." Gerard has been known to call them "majestic." (By the way, bar-goers can enjoy similar porcelain grandeur at P.J. Clarke's and McSorley's.)

Potty talk aside, this throwback, with its wooden booths and 55-foot-long, marble-topped, carved mahogany bar has much to tell. From its

16-foot-high tin ceilings to its antique tiled floor, Old Town reeks of Old World charm. During Prohibition, Tammany Hall pretended not to notice that it served liquor. The restaurant has two floors, with the original working dumbwaiter delivering dishes to and fro. The quieter second floor was once the "Ladies and Gentlemen's Dining Room," with men drinking in the bar below.

One can easily see why Pete Hamill and the brothers McCourt, Frank and Alphie, sought out the place. On a late summer afternoon, the regular customers are gathered around a fellow patron with a ZZ Top beard, all parked on their stools in the front of the bar area beneath the arched windows. The lively après-work crowd, in suits, business casual, and flannel shirts, drink almost anything from liquor on the rocks to rosé, but no one will tease you about your choice of booze. They're too deep in conversation. Frank McCourt observed, "It's the place to talk." He's right. The bartender describes Old Town as a "beer and whiskey kind of place." The bar boasts about its lack of a blender. As for their other mixed drinks, Gerard stated during a priest's blessing of the Nativity scene at the base of the bar's Christmas tree, "We don't water down our traditions, and we don't water down our drinks."

Its walls are covered with framed, signed book jackets and photos of the literati who wet their whistle here: Dermot McEvoy, Billy Collins, Frank McCourt, Christopher Hitchens, Joe Queenan, Budd Schulberg, Pete Hamill (who signed his book jacket for *A Drinking Life*, "For the one bar that still makes me thirsty"), Caleb Carr, and Seamus Heaney. Nick Hornby held his book launch party here. Frank McCourt dropped in often when he taught at Stuyvesant High School and continued to do so once he became a best-selling memoirist.

Pete's Tavern

129 E. 18th Street (between Park Avenue South and 3rd Avenue)
petestavern.com
212-473-7676
Daily: 11 a.m. to 2:30 a.m.

O. Henry, the pen name for William Sidney Porter, may have died in 1910, but more than a century later, he still occupies his favorite booth here, where he spent time writing and drinking. The booth, with its tall wooden backs and intricate carvings, is the second one to the right upon entering. Patrons are welcome to dine and drink in his sanctuary or at the carved rosewood bar. In appreciation of his loyalty, the booth is decorated with O. Henry memorabilia: letters he's written, his last photo, a sign that claims he wrote "The Gift of the Magi" in that very booth in 1905. A plaque posted where he lived, down the street at 55 Irving Place, also claims to being the place where Henry wrote the short story in "two feverish hours." (Porter was a paternal relative of Katherine Anne Porter.)

His story "The Lost Blend," published in 1907, was set in a bar named Kenealey's, modeled after Pete's, which was called Healy's in O. Henry's day until 1932, when Pete Bell bought it: "Con Lantry worked on the sober side of the bar. You and I stood, one-legged like geese, on the other side and went into voluntary liquidation of our week's wages . . .

The saloon (whether blessed or cursed) stood in one of those little 'places' which are parallelograms instead of streets, and inhabited by laundries, decayed Knickerbocker families and Bohemians who have nothing to do with either."

The dark tavern opened on this corner in 1864 and has never ceased operations. It disguised itself as a flower shop during Prohibition, when patrons slinked in through a false refrigerator door.

Much of the tavern's décor is original. The peach-and-robin's-egg-blue tile floor is cracked throughout. The timeworn wooden cashier's cage is tucked at the end of the bar. Above it hangs the original brass gaslight chandelier festooned with small brass angels and original frosted glass globes. Two dining rooms complete the first floor. The Skylight Room, the upstairs dining room, is where *New York Times* best-selling author Rebecca Skloot had the launch party for her book, *The Immortal Life of Henrietta Lacks.* That room once held livestock belonging to Alfred Ringling of Ringling Bros. Circus. He lived on Gramercy Park East. Pete's 1864 House Ale is made upstairs.

Pete's stimulated another writer's creative streak. Austrian immigrant Ludwig Bemelmans, the illustrator and writer, began writing and sketching his Madeline series of children's books on the backs of menus in September 1938. The beloved opening line of each book in the series, "In an old house in Paris that was covered with vines," came to him while sitting in Pete's one afternoon. He, his wife, Madeleine, and his daughter dined nightly at Pete's. They lived nearby in the Hotel Irving. He died of pancreatic cancer at age 64 in his studio apartment in the National Arts Club on Gramercy Park South.

When Johnny Depp was preparing for his movie role as Hunter S. Thompson, he met the Gonzo journalist at Pete's several times.

O. Henry memorabilia adorns a booth.

Thompson, who was particular about the fruit in his cocktails, ordered his frozen daiquiris made with fresh strawberries. If the bar was out of strawberries or other fresh fruit, the waitstaff was sent out to buy them.

Fans of the Harry Potter movies will enjoy checking out the various photos of Daniel Radcliffe.

FROZEN STRAWBERRY
DAIQUIRI

Hunter S. Thompson doesn't seem like a sweet frozen cocktail kind of guy. He rode with the Hell's Angels motorcycle gang for nearly a year as research for his book *Hell's Angels: The Strange and Terrible Saga of the Outlaw Motorcycle Gangs*. The Gonzo journalist—his term for his brand of narrative journalism—played hard, drank hard, drugged hard. Yet he insisted that the bartender at Pete's make his frozen daiquiri with fresh fruit. At dinner with Tom Wolfe in Aspen, he ordered two banana daiquiris and two banana splits for his meal. Upon finishing them, he beckoned to the waitress and requested another round of both the pair of cocktails and the pair of banana splits.

Thompson inveighed against objective journalism because "you can't be objective about [Richard] Nixon," he said. Instead, he blended fiction and fact. His writing was influenced by the works of Mark Twain, Ernest Hemingway, Allen Ginsberg, Jack Kerouac, and Ken Kesey. He developed close friendships with Tom Wolfe, the Beats, and William Kennedy. His signature look entailed a baseball cap and aviator sunglasses, with a cigarette in a holder clenched between his teeth. His most heralded book was *Fear and Loathing in Las Vegas*.

He outlined his typical writing day to an interviewer: "I'd say on a normal day I get up at noon or one. You have to feel sort of overwhelmed, I think, to start. That's what journalism did teach me ... that there is no story unless you've written it." Depending on deadlines, he'd write without stopping for four or five days and nights—likely powered by drugs.

INGREDIENTS

1 cup white rum

1 pint ripe strawberries, hulled

¼ cup fresh lime juice

Superfine sugar, to taste (optional)

Ice cubes

DIRECTIONS

In a blender, add rum, strawberries, lime juice, and about one cup of ice, depending on desired consistency. Pulse to blend. Pour into glass. Add lime wheel. Makes four to six servings, unless a gonzo journalist is imbibing.

Bo's Kitchen & Bar Room

6 W. 24th Street (between 5th and 6th avenues)
bosrestaurant.com/yeahyouwrite
212-234-2373
Lunch: Monday through Friday, 12 to 3 p.m.
Dinner: Monday and Tuesday, 5:30 to 10 p.m.; Wednesday through Saturday
5:30 to 11 p.m.
Bar: Monday through Saturday, 4:30 p.m. to 2 a.m.
Literary-themed cocktails served only at readings. See website for
reading series dates and authors.

A touch of New Orleans food and drink with a New York accent is this eatery's MO, but that's not all this restaurant and bar has to offer. This venue is named after Andrew "Bo" Young III, who has taken up the torch of his father, Civil Rights icon Andrew Young II, as CEO of the charity GiveLocally, based in Atlanta. Bo co-owns this restaurant with partners Todd Mitgang and Steven Kristel. While Bo's family's monkey bread is a draw, the #YeahYouWrite literary reading series brings in top-shelf authors once a month with cocktails to match.

The series is the brainchild of Lisa Kristel and Robin Martin, who met at Salt Cay Writers Workshop in October 2014. A few weeks later over dinner with Martin at Bo's, Kristel pitched an idea for a reading series. After seeing the lounge, Martin signed on to the venture. They kicked off the series in November of the following year with writers Téa Obreht, David Ebershoff, and Dan Sheehan. Obreht's husband, Sheehan, came up with the name for the reading series from the vintage, marquee-style lighted sign, "Yeah You Right," which hangs on one wall in the dining room.

The evenings begin with a presentation of literary-themed cocktails, which are based on an author or book and often include the author's preferred spirits and flavors. Bar manager Peter Marzulli develops each recipe. In the case of Julia Glass, Kristel couldn't resist naming her tequila cocktail "Julia's Glass." Tayari Jones's novel *Silver Sparrow* inspired the "Silver Secret," made with gin, St. Germain, peach, and prosecco, and garnished with a strawberry. "Tired and Emotional," the phrase used by British journalists to describe inebriated politicians and others, was a natural choice for a cocktail served when Christopher Cerf discussed his book *Spinglish: The Definitive Dictionary of Deliberately Deceptive Language*. The euphemism, defined in this reference book, which Cerf coauthored with Henry Beard, came into use to protect journalists from libel suits.

When Glass was asked to read at #YeahYouWrite, she could not say no to traveling from her "brigandoonish town" in New England to New York, where she once lived. "What's not to love about an invitation to return to your beloved New York and costar at a reading series called "YeahYouWrite, held in a subterranean bar called Bo's, where the menu features fried alligator, the bartender will design a cocktail based on your

favorite spirits, [and] you'll get to regal the audience with that story about the worst review you ever received?" The bad review for her first novel, *Three Junes*, appeared in *People*. Her publicist shouted into the phone, "Now you know how Julia Roberts feels!" Glass listened on the other end, tearful while clad in her pajamas in her parents' kitchen. She felt like she was 12 years old all over again. Despite the bad review, her debut novel won the National Book Award for fiction in 2002.

At the outset, each author tastes and assesses the cocktail for the audience. Some have paid tribute to the cocktail in a poem. The readings are followed by a Q&A. "It's a great way to get all the authors speaking and interacting," says Kristel, who serves as the MC while Martin photographs the event. During a break, attendees may purchase books and have them signed. Of course, boozing and schmoozing are encouraged. After the break, audience members may participate in an open mic session. The authors return to recount their worst rejection or reviews. Once the formal part of #YeahYouWrite ends, the participants often linger, indulging in conversation and, perhaps, another cocktail. Dinner is served throughout. Because of limited seating, reservations are required.

Since its debut, the reading series has gained such renown that authors are contacting its coordinators instead of the other way around. Consider these additional literary luminaries who entertained an audience with their works and anecdotes:

Michael Cunningham
Nicole Dennis-Benn
David Ebershoff
Karen Heuhler
Sandra Newman
Daniel José Older
Shelly Oria
Jon Papernick
Austin Ratner
Imani Sims
Anna Solomon

Ratner, following his event, told the series organizer, "These sorts of readings are a meaningful part of the fabric of literary life in New York City, especially when given some care, like you have."

JULIA'S GLASS

Recipe courtesy of Lisa Kristel and Peter Marzulli

The author of the novel *Three Junes*, Julia Glass, is partial to tequila plus citrus and fruit flavors in her cocktails. She also read a travel piece at #YeahYouWrite about her time studying in Italy when she was younger. At #YeahYouWrite, the Twitter-averse Glass, says, "I got a kick out of fraternizing with a hashtag, and best of all, I now have a recipe for a killer cocktail."

INGREDIENTS

1½ ounces tequila

½ ounce pear liqueur

1 ounce fresh lime juice

½ ounce agave syrup

Prosecco

Mint leaves

DIRECTIONS

Shake the tequila, pear liqueur, lime juice, and agave syrup in an ice-filled cocktail shaker. Strain into a flute glass. Top with prosecco and garnish with mint leaves.

Serpent's Nectar

SERPENT'S NECTAR

Recipe courtesy of Lisa Kristel and Peter Marzulli

Poet Kita Shantiris read selections from her book of poetry, *What Snakes Want*. "Thanks to the recipe and Google, I learned that there are male and female coupes—the very male Coupe de Ville and the coupe glass, which has been molded to the shape of beloved breasts for centuries," she told her audience at Bo's. "Lift your coupe with wild abandon."

INGREDIENTS

4 basil leaves

2 cherry tomatoes

2 ounces Spring 44 Mountain Gin

1 ounce fresh lemon juice

½ ounce honey

Freshly ground pepper

DIRECTIONS

Muddle basil and tomatoes in a shaker. Add ice cubes, gin, lemon, and honey. Shake well. Strain into a coupe glass. Slap a basil leaf in the palm of your hand to release the oils. Float it in the glass and top with freshly ground pepper.

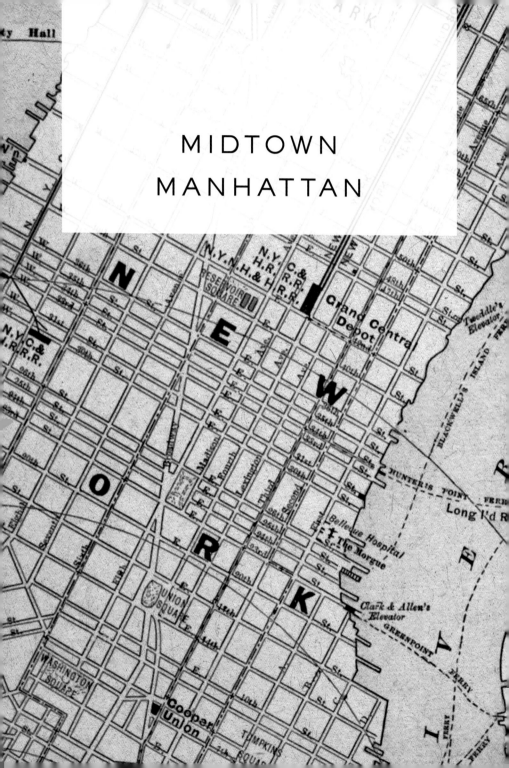

MIDTOWN
MANHATTAN

For the sake of ease, let's establish Manhattan's midsection as encompassing Times Square, Herald Square, and Rockefeller Center. This area stretches between 34th Street and 59th Street from south to north and spans the island's width from the Hudson to the East rivers.

Midtown Manhattan is home to the main branch of New York Public Library, a Beaux-Arts gem guarded by a pair of marble lions, Patience and Fortitude, on Fifth Avenue and 42nd Street. For a walk literally littered with bronze books, traverse 41st Street from Fifth to Park Avenue, christened "Library Way" in the late 1990s. Book-shaped plaques inscribed with quotations on the importance of literature are embedded in the concrete on both sides of the street.

The Algonquin/ Blue Bar

59 W. 44th Street (between 5th and 6th avenues)
algonquinhotel.com
212-840-6800
Round Table: Monday through Friday, 7 to 10:30 a.m.; Saturday and Sunday,
7 to 10 a.m. (breakfast); Sunday, 12 to 3 p.m. (brunch); Daily, 12 to 3 p.m. (lunch);
Sunday through Thursday, 5 to 10:30 p.m.; Friday and Saturday, 5 to 11:30 p.m. (dinner)
Blue Room: daily, 11:30 a.m. to 1 a.m.

No bar existed at the Algonquin when the members of the Round Table began holding their quip-filled lunches at the hotel's restaurant in June 1919. Prohibition wouldn't go into effect until January 17, 1920, but hotelier Frank Case had imposed a "dry blight" of his own in 1917 by shutting down his lobby bar. He grew tired of the cast of characters who had been assembling there for drinks for three years. At first, the kickoff for these unnamed gentlemen's cocktail hour was a reasonable 5 p.m. Then the crew arrived earlier and earlier. He grumbled to his wife about it. By the time their cocktail hour's start time had crept into the morning—and it didn't wind down until late evening—Case cut them off. He wanted no drunks in his lobby, especially because he was raising his children in the family residence upstairs. Frequent diners in the know who wanted to imbibe with their meal, however, could order a drink. Case kept the liquor stored in the pantry. He reopened the bar 16 years later because he was losing money to other hotels and restaurants.

The lack of alcohol didn't perturb Dorothy Parker and Robert Benchley. Neither one of them liked liquor at the time. On the fateful June day in 1919 of that first gathering, they had joined writers, press agents, editors, and newspaper columnists in welcoming *New York Times* drama critic Alexander Woollcott back from World War I. The 4-foot-11-inch Parker spoke little during most of the lunch. When she did utter a vinegar-laced remark, it came out in a voice that was soft and high-pitched, with a touch of a finishing-school accent. John Peter Toohey, a Broadway publicist, suggested that they meet every day, and so the Round Table was born and a decade of bon mots ensued. Initially, they referred to it as the "lunch club," their luncheons "board meetings." They met six days a week.

"I may have been more than a little simple and innocent," Case notes in *Tales of a Wayward Inn*, "for I had no idea that this little knot of young people were so soon to play an important part in the world of books and theater."

Case embraced the group. After all, they garnered publicity for his hotel. They walked from their nearby newspaper, magazine, publishing, and theater offices for their daily lunch and skewering. Case set them up in the Pergola Room (called the Oak Room today). As this close-knit group enlarged, he moved them to the Rose Room (the Round Table Room today), where, in the center, he set a round table that could seat the 25 or so for their ritual lengthy meal. The founding members, in addition

to Woollcott, Parker, and Benchley, were Franklin P. Adams, or F.P.A., the byline he used for his columns; Heywood Broun; Marc Connelly; Jane Grant; Edna Ferber; George S. Kaufman; Harold Ross; and Robert Sherwood, who, because of his 6-foot 8-inch height, was the subject of many wisecracks. Parker remarked once that when she, Sherwood, and the 6-foot Benchley strode down Manhattan's sidewalks together they looked like a "walking pipe organ." Non-writers, including Harpo Marx and Tallulah Bankhead, were sometimes part of their crowd, too.

The group called themselves the "Vicious Circle," while an artist titled his painting of them, *The Algonquin Round Table*. They nicknamed their regular waiter, Luigi, "Luigi Board." (Ouija boards were popular in the twenties.)

During one lunch, Ross and Grant asked their table mates for possible names for a magazine they were planning. Toohey, after inquiring about its

141

intended readership, suggested they call it *The New Yorker* and, without missing a beat, returned to his meal. F.P.A. reported their repartee and goings-on in his columns, which helped the group gain national notoriety.

Other writers longed to join this group, for good reason. The Vicious Circle was the predecessor to the power lunch, albeit an entertaining one. They were networking, helping each other obtain writing assignments and editorial positions, and publishing each other's work. One writer, eager for an entree into the circle, dedicated his novel to 20 of its members, listing them by their initials. He didn't succeed. If he had, we'd know who he was.

Ferber observed that the table had no room for "bores, hypocrites, sentimentalists, or the socially pretentious." If you were pompous or mentally or artistically dishonest, she added, watch out. Ferber writes in her autobiography, *A Peculiar Treasure*, "Their standards were high, their vocabulary fluent, fresh, astringent and very, very tough. Theirs was a tonic influence, one on the other, and all on the world of American letters." Their brand of agile wit laced with cynicism forever changed American humor.

Among their witticisms:

Time wounds all heels. —Frank Case

Satire is something that closes on Saturday night. —George S. Kaufman

Anybody can do any amount of work, provided it isn't what he is supposed to be doing. —Robert Benchley

I told him my funniest story, and he laughed so hard you could hear a pin drop. —Ring Lardner, after meeting President Calvin "Silent Cal" Coolidge

How could they tell? —Dorothy Parker upon hearing news of "Silent Cal's" death

Repartee is what you wish you'd said. —Heywood Broun

Being an old maid is like death by drowning, not an altogether unpleasant sensation after you cease to struggle. —Edna Ferber

In the order named, these are hardest to control—wine, women, and song." —Franklin Pierce Adams

With the Round Table, the hotel and bar's literary pedigree was further cemented. In its early years, William Makepeace Thackeray and Mark Twain, a.k.a. Samuel Clemens, were guests. H. L. Mencken stayed at "The Gonk" during his bimonthly visits to New York from Baltimore.

The Round Table Restaurant is named for Dorothy Parker's famed group.

He was editor of the literary magazine, *The Smart Set*, which was head-quartered in Manhattan. Mencken, though, was not a fan of the Round Table, thinking them frivolous and annoying. He dined elsewhere or held spontaneous parties in his room. He would mix drinks for his guests. During one of Mencken's impromptu boozy parties, Upton Sinclair praised the benefits of fasting and avoiding alcohol.

As for the Round Table's own drinking habits, Prohibition was theirs and many New Yorkers' downfall. Prior to Prohibition, New York City had about 16,000 saloons. By the early 1920s, some 32,000 speakeasies had flourished. Before Prohibition, Parker would nurse one gin daisy for an entire evening at parties. Because the Algonquin no longer had a bar, Broun drank from a flask at the Round Table. Speakeasies were where Parker and Benchley developed their heavy drinking habits. They, like several others in the Vicious Circle, had become alcoholics by the time Prohibition ended in 1933. By then, the Round Table had disbanded.

In 1943, Woollcott, whom James Thurber nicknamed "Old Vitriol and Violets," died of a heart attack. The remnants of the Round Table assembled one last time at the Gonk for a drink and to mourn his passing. Benchley died two years later, Parker in 1967.

A civil rights activist who sympathized with the oppressed, she left her estate to Martin Luther King, Jr., whom she had never met. Her will specified that if something were to happen to him, her estate would go to the NAACP. King was assassinated less than a year after Parker's death. Her ashes, which were kept in her lawyer's file cabinet until 1988, were interred at the NAACP's headquarters in a memorial garden dedicated to her. The plaque's inscription includes her suggested epitaph, "Excuse my dust."

A 1939 guide described the Algonquin as "famed as a literary and stage rendezvous." Gertrude Stein, Alice B. Toklas, and Graham Greene checked in to the hotel on occasion. William Faulkner, who stayed at the hotel three to four times a year, wrote his acceptance speech for the Nobel Prize in 1949 in his room. Maya Angelou, Brendan Behan, John Cheever, Leonard Cohen, William Inge, Norman Mailer, Arthur Miller, J. D. Salinger, William Saroyan, and Tennessee Williams also have been guests. Kurt Vonnegut liked staying at the Algonquin because it was, and remains to this day, "a writer's hotel."

In the twenty-first century, Twitter gave birth to Tweetups, a new way to socialize for publishing types. Bethanne Patrick, Erin McHugh, and I invited the authors, journalists, literary agents, and publishing professionals we'd been conversing with on Twitter to the Round Table for lunch. About 60 people showed up, many of whom had never met in the flesh before. From the laughter, hugging, and conversation, the lunch felt more like a reunion. A waiter asked me how we knew each other. He was astonished at the power of social media. We returned for a Round Table meetup in 2011.

Erika Robuck, who writes historical fiction about the Fitzgeralds, Edna St. Vincent Millay, and Ernest Hemingway, was among the attendees. "Nothing gives me a bigger kick than running my hands along the walls and bars of the Algonquin, hoping that Scott Fitzgerald's or Dorothy Parker's fingerprints still linger," she said. "I have attended two Round Tables at the Algonquin, and there is a certain magic when living—and dead—authors come together."

Robuck would have a hard time finding their fingerprints. In 2012, the hotel's latest owners retrofitted it from top to bottom. They took care to preserve the Gonk's vintage elegance and the integrity of the building while freshening it up. The facade was repaired but otherwise left alone because of its landmark status. The hotel lobby remains the residence of a rescued cat, named either Matilda or Hamlet. Either John Barrymore or Case started that tradition when one of them—no one is sure who— brought in a stray. They named him Hamlet, in the 1920s. (The hotel hosts a cat fashion show every August. This fundraiser, which features some cats dressed in Jazz-Age garb and others dressed as Parker, Benchley, Harpo, and other members of the Round Table, donates the money raised to no-kill animal shelters.)

During the renovation, the new owners also asked Brooklyn artist Natalie Ascencios to paint a second copy of her rendering of the Vicious Circle. Her original painting, commissioned for the hotel's centennial celebration in 2002, was claimed by the corporation that owned the property at the time. The painting, which hangs in the Round Table restaurant, can be seen upon entering this literary landmark. Writers such as Martin Amis and Paul Theroux are still drawn to the hotel.

In keeping with its literary past, the hotel provides e-books to its guests. In the future, the hotel may offer writing residencies. Writers and other guests may hang the hotel's version of the "do not disturb" sign on their door: "Quiet Please. Writing the Great American Novel." The Dorothy Parker Society meets here on Fridays during the summer.

Visitors in search of literary-themed cocktails may order one in the lobby or the Blue Bar.

THE DOROTHY PARKER

Recipe courtesy of the Algonquin

The Algonquin's Blue Bar would be remiss if it didn't serve a cocktail named after Dottie. The Blue Bar takes its name from its blue lighting, a recommendation by actor John Barrymore. He told Case that blue gels are placed over stage lights because they make people look good. With that advice, Case installed blue lighting in the bar.

This recipe was created for the Blue Bar by Allen Katz, general manager of the New York Distilling Company.

INGREDIENTS

2 to 3 ounces gin
½ ounce St. Germain
½ ounce fresh lemon juice
Honey to taste
Basil leaves

DIRECTIONS

Add all liquid ingredients to a cocktail shaker filled with ice. Stir or shake. Pour into chilled glass. Garnish with basil.

The Dorothy Parker cocktail won't set you back like the hefty $10,000 bar bill for the hotel's special martini would. A person looking to propose to a beloved may arrange beforehand for the bartender to serve that cocktail garnished with a sparkling piece of "ice," as in, a diamond. An in-house jeweler will help you and your intended select a setting.

21

21 W. 52nd Street (between Fifth and Sixth avenues)
21club.com
212-582-7200
Bar Room: Monday through Friday, 12 to 2:30 p.m. (lunch); Monday through Thursday, 5:30 to 10 p.m. (dinner); Friday, 5:30 to 11 p.m. (dinner); Saturday, 5 to 11 p.m. (dinner)
Bar 21 and Lounge: Monday through Friday, 12 p.m. to close; Saturday, 5 p.m. to close

---

"Write what you know" may be cliché advice, but authors nevertheless like to set scenes from their novels in their favorite drinking haunts. In the opening of Dashiell Hammett's *The Thin Man*, Nick awaits his wife, Nora, at a speakeasy on West 52nd Street. He orders Scotch and sodas at the bar—one for himself and one for a woman of mystery. Although about 38 speakeasies lined that block, Nick and Nora fans like to believe that Hammett had 21 in mind. Hammett himself would drop in for drinks with his buddy William Faulkner in 1931, two years before *The Thin Man* was published.

Nearly two decades later, long after 21's speakeasy days, Truman Capote had come to favor the bar. Around the time he began his brief stint as a copyboy for *The New Yorker* in the early 1940s, Capote also started having 21's meals delivered to his apartment. In *Breakfast at Tiffany's*, his narrator spots Holly Golightly at a table with four men.

Her yawning, along with her combing her hair at the table, the narrator says, put "a dampener on the excitement I felt over dining at so swanky a place."

The 21 has been the darling of the literary world ever since its days in Greenwich Village. The secret to its early success as a speakeasy involved relocating often, renaming the bar with each move so as to keep ahead of the federal agents, and getting in on the good side of each new location's police department. The owners went one step further: Bathtub gin was verboten—only excellent food and high-quality liquor, wine, and champagne from trusted bootleggers could be served.

In the early days of Prohibition, two cousins, Jack Kriendler from the Lower East Side and Charles Berns of the Upper West Side, ditched their college studies to open a "speak." They hoped to fund their education with the profits. Charlie had misgivings about their entrepreneurial venture. Jack, meanwhile, drew in a partner, Edward Irving, and persuaded friends and family to invest in their enterprise. In 1922, they found a spot on 6th Avenue and W. 4th Street and named it the "Red Head." The speakeasy was disguised as a tearoom, with liquor served in teacups. They kept gangsters away from their popular speak and, with a little moola, enlisted police protection. At that point, Charlie rejoined the business.

Because Jack envisioned a classier joint, they moved to 88 Washington Place on the corner of 6th Avenue after greasing the palms of another precinct. They called it "Frontón," the décor of which was a step up from the Red Head's divey atmosphere. To keep out the riffraff, the front door had a peep hole so that patrons could be screened. If federal agents, or "booze busters," paid them a visit, someone would ring a buzzer to warn that a raid was imminent. Patrons were instructed, "bottoms up." After gulping down their gin, rye, bourbon, or Scotch, they sprinted out a back door. All alcohol would be tossed down the drain. The feds would look around and see no alcohol. The stench of alcohol was not enough for the feds to bring criminal charges.

Edna St. Vincent Millay, who lived in Greenwich Village, and Dorothy Parker went there for drinks, as did James "Jimmie" Walker, mayor of New York. Flappers and college students joined in the merriment.

A planned subway line forced 21 to find new digs again. In 1926, eyeing the many well-to-do people who were taking up residence in Midtown Manhattan, the owners found a toney townhouse property with an ornamental iron gate located at 42 W. 49th Street. This time, their speak was called "The Puncheon Grotto." People, including the owners, referred to it as "The Puncheon," "The Grotto," or "Jack and Charlie's." They hoped to attract an upscale clientele: a place where men of letters, of wealth, could bring their wives or dates. Jack wanted to create a comfortable atmosphere where people could linger, talk, or read the newspaper.

In *The Speakeasies of 1932*, Al Hirschfeld writes that 21 was "frequented by writers of the better order; the cosmopolite; the men who go to the nearby picture galleries; understand Matisse, Ravel, and Ernest Bloch; who know *canard a la presse*, drink hock, and call for their whiskey by name." Soon Robert Benchley was bringing his Round Table crowd to his new discovery after their luncheons at the Algonquin. At 21 they'd run into Ernest Hemingway, Ben Hecht, Charles MacArthur, and John O'Hara.

Plans for Rockefeller Center in 1930 put the kibosh on this spot. On New Year's Eve, 1929, the owners held a demolition party, serving mint juleps, made with gin, and planter's punch. The carousers, Benchley among them, wielding sledgehammers, pickaxes, crowbars, and other ersatz tools, tore down walls, broke up flooring, and otherwise reduced the place to rubble. They proved Benchley's witticism: "Drinking makes such fools of people, and people are such fools to begin with, that it's compounding a felony." The demolition done, a policeman joined in the mirth and rode his horse through the debris.

They carried dinnerware, chairs, cookware, and even the iron gate to their final and current location, 21 W. 52nd Street, that night. Lunch was served at the new address on the first day of 1930. Although two of the moves were due to circumstances beyond their control, the frequent name changes ensured that the bar would leave no money trail behind, which helped its owners to elude the feds.

At the new location, gangsters and the police left them untouched, except once. Gossip columnist Walter Winchell was miffed that he was *persona non grata* at this watering hole. The speakeasy, with its numerous journalists, editors, publicists, writers, and Broadway and movie stars, would have provided much fodder for his columns. In 1932, Winchell sought revenge—in ink. In his column, he asked why 21 had never been raided by the feds. They turned up the next day, but the warrant they brought with them was flawed, and as a result, the feds could do little but give them a mild reprimand.

Fearing that they wouldn't be as lucky the second time around, the owners sought out an architect to design several means to foil the feds. They devised an elaborate security system that entailed false staircases and walls, secret alarms, bar shelves that would collapse at the push of a button, dumping all the bottles through a chute where they'd shatter, and a camouflaged vault in the cellar that could be opened only by inserting a spaghetti-thin wire into a hard-to-find hole. Once the wire completed

The Bar Room

the electrical circuit, the door could be pushed open. The vault door was disguised with brick to match the surrounding the wall, which made it heavy. During Prohibition, Mayor Jimmy Walker had a private booth in the basement vault, with a personal telephone line to receive calls from municipal offices. The ruses extended to their bootleggers, one of whom delivered his goods in a hearse. Others stashed bottles of booze under car fenders. Their efforts turned out to be unnecessary: 21 was never subject to another raid.

Jack, who was fascinated with the Old West, often greeted guests such as F. Scott Fitzgerald in Western garb. H. L. Mencken may have wanted nothing to do with the members of the Round Table while staying at the Algonquin, but he didn't mind running into them at 21, his boîte of choice when he was in town. He did, however, prefer to sit with others.

Over the years, the dining area, bar and lounge, and wine cellar vault acquired unique characteristics. Unlike restaurant chains with faux scratchy antique trinkets and faded signs, 21 came by its collection honestly. The walls are crammed with *New Yorker* cartoons and photos of famous patrons accumulated over the years. In the main room, memorabilia gifted to the bar by patrons dangles from the ceiling: model airplanes and trucks, Dorothy Hamill's ice skates, a Julia Child cookbook, Willie Mays's baseball bat, George Plimpton's book of interviews of Truman Capote's friends, lovers, and colleagues. Given Jack's predilection for all things Western, Remington sculptures and paintings are mounted throughout.

The outside of the building stands out, too. Since the thirties, 21 has catered to the horsey set, who donated colorful miniature cast-iron lawn jockeys denoting the colors of their respective horse farms. To date, 34 jockeys adorn the ironwork and steps, the most recent one being a jockey representing Zayat Stables, which owns the 2015 Triple Crown winner, American Pharaoh.

Author anecdotes involving this celebrated watering hole are plentiful. It is here that Benchley is said to have uttered, one rainy night, "Get me out of this coat and into a wet martini." Seeing Ernest Hemingway arrive, the bartender would prepare a "Papa doble," a double daiquiri consisting of white rum, juice of two limes and half a grapefruit, and six maraschino cherries. The Papa doble was created for Hemingway by a bartender in Cuba. Papa Hemingway sometimes would shake his head no and tell the 21 bartender, "Since I'm not drinking, I'll just have a tequila." Hemingway was like a father to Bob, the son of 21 founder

Jack, who died in 1947. When writer Gene Fowler was hospitalized, Bob snuck a bottle of Scotch into his room. Fowler inscribed his next novel, *Salute to Yesterday*, "To my timely young friend, who rushed into battle and thereby saved my life."

Bob loved novels and the authors who wrote them. Under his sway, 21 started collecting books authored by their patrons. Bob would have them sign two books—one for himself and one to be donated to the Rutgers University Library. One day, Bob asked Hemingway if John Steinbeck might inscribe one of his books. Hemingway urged the aloof Steinbeck to sign it. When Steinbeck asked Hemingway what he should write, Hemingway told him to write something scatological. The inscription? "To Bob Kriendler, Scatologically, John Steinbeck." Steinbeck later signed a first edition of *The Portable Steinbeck*, a collection of his works, "Bob—It's a little tiny world as we both know—*pas de merde.* John Steinbeck."

Other authors and journalists who got by those iron gates for a place at tables shrouded in red-checkered tablecloths were Lillian Hellman (who was romantically involved with Hammett), Harold Ross, Sinclair Lewis, Somerset Maugham, H.G. Wells, Edward R. Murrow, Studs Terkel, Peter Benchley (son of Robert), Brendan Gill, John Updike, and Helen Gurley Brown. Ludwig Bemelmans, author and illustrator of the Madeline children's books, wrote in a letter, "I would like to be buried in 21's cellar, with the Kriendlers standing by in dark suits, each holding a burning candle in one hand, and in the other my large bills." A World War II army veteran, Bemelmans is buried in Arlington National Cemetery.

When Benchley died in 1945, the bar held a memorial for him. A bronze plaque marks Benchley's preferred corner booth.

The wine cellar is a liquid archive of Prohibition itself. Dusty bottles of gin dating to Prohibition fill the shelves, next to the private wine collections of Nelson Doubleday, the publisher, and Sidney Sheldon, the author of steamy best-sellers, as well as U.S. presidents, movie stars and directors, plus two business tycoons who served time in a federal penitentiary. Because many of the owners of these collections are deceased, the bottles belong to their estate. Tasting parties of up to 20 people can dine and drink in the wine cellar. The current owner added a custom table in honey-colored wood. It has an inlaid pair of jockeys flanking the number "21" in the center.

SOUTHSIDE FIZZ

Recipe courtesy of 21

While Manhattans and martinis are the most frequently requested drinks here, 21 has been serving this cocktail since the 1930s. It pairs well with seafood dishes. To evoke that era, sip this while listening to classics from 21's playlist, the Great American Songbook.

INGREDIENTS

2 ounces gin *(Tanqueray is recommended)*
1 ounce mint simple syrup
4 to 5 fresh mint leaves
Juice of one lemon
Splash of club soda

DIRECTIONS

Place all ingredients in a mixing glass and shake vigorously to bruise mint leaves. Strain into a collins glass filled with ice. Finish with a splash of soda.

The Monkey Bar

60 E. 54th Street (between Madison and Park avenues)
monkeybarnewyork.com
212-288-1010
Monday through Friday: 11:30 a.m. to 10 p.m.
Saturday: 5:30 to 10 p.m.
Bar open till 1 a.m.

The lore of how the Monkey Bar acquired its moniker comes in three versions. The original bar, which opened in 1936 in the Hotel Elysée lobby, was known as the Elysée Bar and Lounge. The dimly lit lounge featured a small stage for a piano and a bar with room for just four stools. In the first version, the story goes that round mirrors with monkey decals were positioned at 25-degree angles above the banquettes. Given the mirrors' angles, patrons could see each other's reflections and were inspired to make faces at each other. In other words, monkey faces. The bawdy piano acts laced with double-entendres—Walter Winchell deemed them "risgay [*sic*] ditties"—might have egged them on.

The second tale involves the actress Tallulah Bankhead, who lived at the hotel for 18 years, held wild parties, and kept an array of pets, including a mynah, a lion cub, and yes, a monkey. The monkey accompanied her to the bar, and while she was hitting the sauce, the monkey roamed the bar. Bankhead always told the bartender taking her order,

"Just tell Mr. [Mayer] Quain [the hotelier] this is on the house."

Hanky-panky imbues the plot line of the final christening story. Executives in the neighborhood would often take mistresses to the bar for cocktails before getting a room. The hotel's reputation as a place for assignations earned it the nickname, "Hotel Easy Lay"—the place for monkey business. (A 1975 *Harper's Bazaar* story, "Should You Sleep With Your Boss?," suggested the Elysée: "Go directly to this underpublicized hotel.")

After Quain died in 1944, his son, Leon, had the bar renovated and enlarged. The mirrors were replaced with a campy mural, painted by a caricaturist, that depicts monkeys playing golf and cards, opening birthday presents, riding an elephant, and, as real chimps do, cavorting in trees. Sections of the mural have been retouched or covered a few times because of subsequent renovations over the decades. Large sconces featuring simians in various poses (the sconce behind the host desk features a monkey reading a book), which were cast in France in the 1940s, provide soft lighting. Imagine what the droll Robert Benchley or Dorothy Parker

The Mercer	WOrth 6-6060
The Four Seasons Hotel	PLaza 8-5700
The Algonquin	TIllinghast 0-6800
The Pierre	TEmpleton 8-8000
The Waldorf-Astoria	EL Dorado 5-3000
The City Club	WAdsworth 1-5500
The Waverly Inn & Garden	N/A
The Oyster Bar	HVacinth 0-6650
La Grenouille	PLaza 2-1495
The '21' Club	LUxembourg 2-7200
The Four Seasons	PLaza 4-9494
Da Silvano	YUkon 2-2343
Elaine's	LEhigh 4-8103
Patroon	TUlip 3-7373
The Brook	PLaza 3-7020
The Racquet Club	PLaza 3-9700
The Union League Club	LIberty 5-3800

would say about these monkeys when they dropped in for booze and bawdy tunes. Ben Hecht liked this particular gin mill, as did F. Scott Fitzgerald.

By the 1980s, the hotel and bar had lost their sheen. In 1983, they appeared on people's radar, but for a sad reason. Frequent resident Tennessee Williams, who was dependent on prescription drugs, choked on the cap of a medication bottle and died in his room a few floors above the bar.

In 1992, the bar was closed without notice. It reopened in 1994 under new ownership. They resuscitated it while preserving the murals and the sconces, but the Monkey Bar still struggled. The bar was rescued again in 2008, when *Vanity Fair* editor Graydon Carter, his wife, and hotelier Jeff Klein purchased it. They commissioned Ed Sorel to paint a wraparound mural in the back room that pays homage to literary lights, composers and musicians, jazz icons, stars of Broadway and film, and publishers. They commissioned more simian lighting: Monkeys form the bases of small table lamps tucked here and there. They restored it to its original glamour, only more so. Think Jazz Age meets posh club. With its literary history, no wonder authors choose the Monkey Bar for their book launch parties.

In this swish yet playful oasis, with traditional jazz playing in the background, imagine drinking a Monkey Gland with Robert Benchley, Tennessee Williams, or James Clavell. Consider Harold Robbins, who cranked out novels that sizzled with sex, money, and power, taking a break from writing four of his best-sellers in an upstairs hotel room. One could easily imagine Robbins, known as a Casanova who lived life in the fast lane, carrying on with a woman on a banquette—and giving gossip columnists something to tattle about.

Peruse Sorel's mural and test your literary knowledge. Here's who to look for in the lineup:

Robert Benchley
Edna Woolman Chase
Edna Ferber
F. Scott Fitzgerald
Zelda Fitzgerald

Ernest Hemingway

Langston Hughes

George S. Kaufman

Alfred A. Knopf

Blanche Knopf

Clare Booth Luce

Henry Luce

Elsa Maxwell

Condé Nast

Eugene O'Neill

Adolph Ochs

Clifford Odets

Dorothy Parker

Harold Ross

Tennessee Williams

Walter Winchell

Alexander Woollcott

MONKEY GLAND

Recipe courtesy of the Monkey Bar

The original cocktail was inspired by a bizarre medical procedure popular in the 1920s. A French surgeon grafted tissue from monkey testicles onto men's testicles in order to enhance their virility and longevity. He didn't stop there, but we'll leave out his other barbaric experiments in xenotransplantation. Besides, no other cocktails pay homage to his dubious enterprises. E. E. Cummings mentions the French surgeon in "XVIII," from his poetry collection *is 5*: "it is the famous doctor who inserts / monkeyglands in millionaires a cute idea n'est-ce pas?"

A bartender also had a sense of humor about the monkey glands, though. The drink's creator is said to be Harry McElhone, proprietor of the famed Harry's New York Bar in Paris. You can thank him for the Bloody Mary, the sidecar, and the French 75, too.

Here's Julie Reiner's take on this classic cocktail. Reiner developed the Monkey Bar's cocktail program.

INGREDIENTS

2 ounces London dry gin

¾ ounce fresh orange juice

½ ounce simple syrup

¼ ounce fresh lemon juice

1 bar spoon pomegranate molasses

2 dashes absinthe

2 dashes orange bitters

2 brandy-soaked Luxardo cherries for garnish

DIRECTIONS

Place ingredients in a cocktail shaker filled with ice. Shake vigorously. Strain into a chilled martini glass. Garnish with two brandy-soaked Luxardo cherries. Do not substitute the Luxardo cherries with maraschino cherries.

The Monkey Gland

P.J. Clarke's

915 Third Avenue (cross street: 55th Street)
pjclarkes.com
212-317-1616
Daily: 11:30 a.m. to 4 a.m.

Charles Jackson's semi-autobiographical novel, *The Lost Weekend*, published in 1944, tells the story of Don Birnam's epic five-day bender, some of which takes place at a bar very much like P.J. Clarke's. *The New York Times Book Review* judged it "the most compelling gift to the literature of addiction since [Thomas] De Quincey." Jackson, an alcoholic, patronized this bar. Director Billy Wilder adapted the book for a movie, which netted four Academy Awards, including Best Picture and Best Director. The Hollywood set for "Nat's Bar" was such a faithful replica of P.J. Clarke's that Robert Benchley, who was also an actor, went to the set every day at 5 p.m. on the dot. Homesick for New York City and for P.J. Clarke's, he would sip a glass of bourbon and depart.

Patrick Joseph Clarke and his family owned this Victorian red brick saloon for 69 years. Clarke had taken it over in 1912 from the original proprietor, an Englishman who opened it in 1884 but then decided to return to England for a "proper wife." The building had been built in 1868 on a lot occupied by squatter shacks. The location under the 3rd

Avenue El (the elevated subway) attracted tannery, brewery, and construction workers on their way home.

A devout Catholic and family oriented, Clarke banned prostitutes and the criminal element from his establishment. Patrons were expected to refrain from using profanities. Forget any notions of getting drunk or gambling, too.

During Prohibition, he put bottles of soda on display, but clued-in patrons knew the room in which alcohol was served. So did the cops and Mayor Jimmy Walker, a "wet," a.k.a. an opponent of Prohibition. As with many Irish bars, women were welcome, but they had to enter through a side door—even Marilyn Monroe, who met Truman Capote for drinks there on occasion. That tradition disappeared in the sixties.

In addition to its movie appearances, the bar has been shouted out by authors and illustrators. In the 1969 novel *The Love Machine*, by Jacqueline Susann, one character orders the renowned burger and a few drinks. (Nat King Cole proclaimed the bar's cheeseburger to be "the

Cadillac of burgers.") *The New Yorker* featured P.J. Clarke's on the cover of its November 27, 1971, issue. Characters in a few Mary Higgins Clark novels stop in for a burger or a drink. To see the real P.J. Clarke's in a movie, watch *The Insider,* based on a true story about a tobacco company whistleblower, and don't blink. Pete Hamill makes a cameo appearance standing at the bar.

The El was torn down in the fifties, leading to real estate grabs along 3rd Avenue. One real estate developer had his eyes on the block where P.J. Clarke's stood. Then-owners the Lavezzos refused any offers, with celebrities such as Johnny Carson joining the battle to save the land-mark. They prevailed. A black skyscraper towers over the short red-brick tavern, which continues to hug its little corner.

Jacqueline Kennedy, who worked at a nearby publishing house, would occasionally drop in for a meal, usually a burger. She sometimes held working lunches there with authors and editors. Mario Vargas Llosa supped on eggs Benedict and a Bloody Mary whenever he was in town. Brendan Behan used to write here undisturbed, often with his typewriter. Eugene O'Neill took his whiskey at the bar, possibly studying the por-trait of Abraham Lincoln. Hamill dined here often, sometimes in the company of Ava Gardner and Frank Sinatra. Gay and Nan Talese appear now and again.

In 2002, restaurateur Philip Scotti, along with actor Timothy Hutton and New York Yankees owner George Steinbrenner, bought P.J. Clarke's. "I used to be a customer," Scotti says. "It was my 'first date' place. If she didn't get it, she was too fancy for me." They purchased the bar for what it stood for, with few plans to change its character. They closed it for a much-needed restoration. One wall required reinforcement, and every-thing needed a deep cleaning.

However, everything that gave it character remained intact: from the pair of human femurs—an Irish talisman for good luck, except, one supposes, for the original owner of the bones—hanging above the entryway between the bar and dining room to the ashes belonging to Phil Kennedy, a frequent customer and baseball infielder for the St. Louis Cardinals. The infamous tall urinals remain. Sinatra once kidded that the 5-foot-2-inch New York City Mayor Abraham Beame could live in one with room to spare. "I love the idea of an American saloon," Scotti says. "We're a little irreverent."

Also intact is the purpose of the bar. "Our job is to help them talk to each other," Scotti says. One sign posted: "Talk to the table next to you. If they don't talk back, we'll throw them out." Staff members are required to get to know one thing about each customer they serve.

P.J. Clarke's teems throughout with old-school ambience: waitstaff in black ties and white shirts hustling about, their classic floor-length French white aprons flapping with each step, crisp white tablecloths with red-and-white checkered tablecloths layered on top, wood paneling, penny floor tile, carved mahogany bar, stained glass, and brown tin ceiling. *New York Times* reporter Frank Bruni called it "a living diorama of a certain era and sensibility." A bartender told Bruni that he considers it "the Vatican of saloons."

The El no longer drowns out the conversation at the bar, but on any weekday night, the din at P.J. Clarke's electrifies this watering hole. Rising over the noise, you might hear such tidbits as "We'll talk about it when we're hammered," or one friend telling his friend, "It's a guys weekend and you're bringing your girlfriend? Dude, you're married."

Says Scotti, "I love my bar."

OLD FASHIONED

Recipe courtesy of P.J. Clarke's

At P.J. Clarke's, this old fashioned is a best-seller. The bar has a philosophy about its cocktail program. The spirits are meant to enhance the cocktails rather than be hidden under a profusion of fruit.

INGREDIENTS

1 sugar cube or 1 teaspoon granulated sugar

Aromatic bitters

1 teaspoon water

1 Amarena cherry

2 ounces artisanal bourbon

Half-moon orange slice

DIRECTIONS

Place a sugar cube in the bottom of a rocks glass. Add three drops of the bitters and a teaspoon of water. Drop in the Amarena cherry. Muddle until the sugar is dissolved. Add three to four ice cubes. Stir. Add the bourbon and stir again. Float a half-moon slice of orange in the glass.

Bedford & Co./ The Renwick

118 E. 40th Street (between Park and Lexington avenues)
bedfordandco.com
therenwickhotelnewyork.com
212-634-4040 (Bedford & Co.)
212-687-4875 (The Renwick)
Breakfast: daily, 7 to 10:30 a.m.
Brunch: Saturday and Sunday, 11:30 a.m. to 3:30 p.m.
Lunch: weekdays, 11:30 a.m. to 3:30 p.m.
Sunset menu: weekdays, 3:30 to 5 p.m.
Dinner: Monday through Saturday, 5:30 to 11 p.m.; Sunday, 5:30 to 11 p.m.
Bar opens daily at 11:30 a.m.

This former extended-stay building, the Hotel Bedford, which was built in 1928, catered to writers (and artists) who needed a place to park their typewriters and to crash for anywhere from a few weeks to a few years. Luminaries John Steinbeck, Ernest Hemingway, and F. Scott Fitzgerald slept here. Children's author Gertrude Crownfield lived here until her death in 1945.

Steinbeck opens his travel book *The Russian Journal* with a scene in its bar. He is talking to war photographer Robert Capa. "A play I had written four times had melted and run out between my fingers. I sat on the bar stool wondering what to do next," Steinbeck writes. Over "two pale green Suissesses," a nineteenth-century New Orleans cocktail made with absinthe, the pair decide to venture to Russia and report on the lives of Russians under Stalin. The book was published with photographs taken by Capa.

Thomas Mann and his wife, in exile from their native Germany, made the Hotel Bedford their first American refuge for a few days in 1938. Mann, a pacifist, had fled from Zurich, where he first lived in exile, to America because he wanted to escape "the poisoned atmosphere of [Hitler's] Germany." Mann knew the hotel well. Whenever he came to New York City to give talks, he stayed at the Hotel Bedford.

The hotel underwent an extensive rehab and reopened in 2015 as a boutique hotel named after James Renwick, the architect of St. Patrick's Cathedral, who resided at the Hotel Bedford. The hotel and bar pay tribute to its former author-denizens.

Bedford and Co., which is not owned by the hotel but connects directly to its lobby, offers cocktails linked to scribes, such as Steinbeck's potable of choice, the Jack Rose, or Hemingway's daiquiri. Hotel guests can order an $85 cocktail, The Gatsby, and have it delivered to their author-themed rooms, where the walls are stenciled with quotations. (Alternately, they can order the Proibito, its cousin, at the bar for much less.) The Thomas Mann suite has patterned wallpaper that evokes mountains. Desk blotters are imprinted with the stain from the bottom of a glass, presumably a cocktail, with a quotation often attributed to Papa Hemingway, "Write drunk." The complete quote is "Write drunk. Edit sober." However, the source may be the novel *Reuben, Reuben*, which was written by Peter de Vries and published in 1970. Chapter Thirty begins with a character based on Dylan Thomas saying, "Sometimes I write drunk and revise sober, and sometimes I write sober and revise drunk."

On the wall next to the lobby entrance to Bedford and Co., a wall of doodles by Brooklyn-born artist Gregory Siff celebrates the authors and painters who've stayed and drank at the hotel and bar.

The Zelda

THE ZELDA

Recipe courtesy of Bedford & Co.

This cocktail tantalizes taste buds with a sweet, sour, and spicy kick, just like its namesake, Zelda Sayre Fitzgerald, Southern belle and wife of F. Scott. A vivacious woman, Zelda was known as "America's First Flapper." She dispensed with Victorian values and embraced a life of self-indulgence and wild abandon. In a 1919 letter to F. Scott, she wrote, "All I want is to be very young always and very irresponsible and to feel that my life is my own."

Chef John DeLucie, formerly with the Waverly Inn (a Greenwich Village bar and restaurant owned by *Vanity Fair* editor Graydon Carter), crafted this cocktail for Zelda, who also stayed at the Hotel Bedford. Lead bartender Tommy Warren says, "We decided to dedicate this cocktail to the frequently wild Zelda herself, as we all have a tequila story of our own."

INGREDIENTS

2 ounces Cimarron blanco tequila

1 ounce fresh grapefruit juice

½ ounce fresh lime juice

½ ounce Cointreau

1 disc-shaped slice jalapeño, seeds removed

DIRECTIONS

Place ingredients in a shaker filled with ice. Shake well and strain into a glass filled with ice. Add a fresh disc of jalapeño.

Charlie Palmer at The Knick

6 Times Square (Broadway and 42nd Street)
theknickerbocker.com
212-204-4983
Breakfast: 7 to 11 a.m.
Lunch: 11:30 a.m. to 2 p.m.
Dinner: 5 to 10 p.m.
Bar and lounge service: 11 a.m. to midnight
Cocktail service: 3 p.m. to midnight

Stand at the fast-paced intersection of 42nd Street and Broadway and travel back in time to the last decade of the nineteenth century. The roads were unpaved, rutted, and littered with animal dung. A horse farm stood at the intersection, along with thickets of trees and berry bushes. Turkeys, bears, and beavers roamed the area, quenching their thirst at a stream that crossed it. By then, city planners had laid out the Manhattan street grid, setting 42nd Street as a major east-west thoroughfare, cutting through Longacre Square. John Jacob Astor, a wealthy furrier, bought this prime real estate because he could envision the future of this nearly bucolic setting. And it was good.

He leased the lot to the builder of the St. Cloud Hotel, which stood there for 20 years until it was razed in 1902. In 1903, construction began on a much larger hotel. Three years later, Astor's great grandson, John Jacob Astor IV, opened The Knickerbocker, a French Renaissance–style building. The new hotel became an overnight sensation in an area that was now home to theaters and the new headquarters of *The New York Times*. The luxury hotel had 556 rooms and, on the first three floors, several restaurants and bars. With all its amenities and shops, the hotel became a playground for the rich and famous, William Randolph Hearst, Mary Pickford, and Enrico Caruso among them. They called it "The Knick," and regulars referred to themselves as members of the "Forty-Second Street Country Club."

For the main bar's centerpiece, Astor hired Maxfield Parrish to paint a 30-foot mural illustrating the nursery rhyme "Old King Cole." Parrish, a Quaker, resisted taking on a commission to do a painting for a drinking establishment, but Astor won—maybe. Parrish caved when Astor offered him five grand, but Parrish may have had the last word. He made King Cole seem greatly diminished in an oversized throne. Word has it that the small face might be Astor's. The mural drew many patrons to the bar, making it an even more popular watering hole than ever.

One of those patrons was F. Scott Fitzgerald. "The Knickerbocker Bar, beamed upon by Maxfield Parrish's jovial, colorful 'Old King Cole,' was well crowded," he wrote in his debut novel, *This Side of Paradise*. Fitzgerald stayed at the hotel in 1919, writing his short story "Mr. Icky" in his room. He would dine with his then girlfriend, Zelda Sayre, in the restaurant. An inebriated Fitzgerald—inebriated, no doubt from too many gin rickeys, his tipple of choice—gained notoriety at the bar because he would fling 20- and 50-dollar bills around. (For a different take on the hotel during the early twentieth century, readers might dip into Clive Cussler's Isaac Bell series. The detectives' offices are located at the Knick.)

Prohibition put a damper on the party that was The Knickerbocker. Vincent Astor, the son of John Jacob Astor IV (who perished in 1912 on the *Titanic* following his honeymoon), converted the hotel into an office building. In 1932, the mural was reinstalled at another Astor property, the St. Regis Hotel, where it can be seen today, in the King Cole Bar. In the forties, *Newsweek* had its offices in the former hotel. In 1980, the advent of a commercial real estate collapse prompted its then owners to convert the building into residential lofts. Once the commercial real estate market turned around, the rooms were rented to Garment District companies as showrooms and offices.

The building changed hands a few more times until 2012, when hotel investors from Dubai bought the building. They had the building gutted, leaving the facade, which is listed on the National Register of Historic Places, intact. The latest owners reopened the hotel in 2015, reinstating its original moniker and commemorating its former glory while lending an ultra-modern style, befitting a twenty-first-century hotel, to its interior.

The hotel has two bars. Charlie Palmer's at The Knick is located on the fourth floor overlooking the corner of 42nd Street and Broadway. The cocktail menu pays tribute to the building's history and legends with drinks including the Knickerbocker Martini and the Astor 400. (The latter is a reference to the social register of 400 prominent and well-heeled New Yorkers kept by Caroline Astor, wife of William and sister-in-law of Mrs. John Jacob Astor IV. While only 309 were invited to attend her "Patriarchal Balls," the "400" moniker stuck.) The ambience of the lounge and bar whispers luxe with its mocha leather armchairs and

couches and metal curtains. The wall of liquor bottles is illuminated from behind, casting a multicolored glow on the bar. Most weekday evenings, the lounge has live jazz performers.

For a dazzling view of Times Square, head for the St. Cloud, the rooftop bar—the only one in the area. The former headquarters of Condé Nast is across the way on 42nd Street.

THE KNICK MARTINI

Recipe courtesy of Charlie Palmer at The Knick

A legend took root that the martini was invented by one Knickerbocker bartender named "Martini di Arma di Taggia," who served the now-classic cocktail to John D. Rockefeller. The oil tycoon drank it regularly and christened it "Martini." Despite this legend, the much-written-about martini could never have originated at this watering hole. William F. Mulhall, who reigned over the Grand Saloon at the elegant Hoffman House Hotel on 25th Street and Broadway, wrote about mixing martinis for his gentleman customers—the bar was males only—in the 1880s. Some cocktail sleuths date the alluring drink to a decade or two before that. Nevertheless, the reincarnated Knickerbocker alludes to its alleged claim to cocktail fame on its menu with a version that is stirred, not shaken.

INGREDIENTS

2 ounces artisanal London dry gin

¾ ounce dry vermouth

½ ounce sweet vermouth

Dash orange bitters

Dash citrus bitters

Lemon peel garnish

DIRECTIONS

Combine the gin, dry vermouth, and sweet vermouth in a mixing glass. Add the bitters and ice. Stir. Pour into a martini glass, while ensuring that the ice remains in the mixing glass. Add lemon peel garnish.

GIN RICKEY

Jazz Age author F. Scott Fitzgerald was so enamored of the Gin Rickey that he made it Jay Gatsby's favorite refreshment, too.

The Gin Rickey also has a murky origin story. Rickeys, be they gin, whiskey, or brandy, could be the 1883 invention of a Missouri politician named Joe Rickey, who used them to cool off on hot summer days while living in Washington, DC. The alternate story has it that the bartender of Shoomaker's, a dive bar in DC, mixed it up for Rickey on a daily basis.

INGREDIENTS

2 ounces London dry gin

Juice of half a lime

Soda water

Lime twist or wedge

DIRECTIONS

Place gin and lime juice in an ice-filled highball or wine glass. Add soda water to fill. Stir. Add garnish.

King Cole Bar/ St. Regis Hotel

2 East 55th Street (cross street: Fifth Avenue)
stregisnewyork.com
212-753-4500
Monday through Saturday: 11:30 a.m. to 1 a.m.
Sunday: 12 p.m. to midnight

———

An English nursery rhyme comes to life in the back of the lobby of the St. Regis. After a brief period in storage during Prohibition, Maxfield Parrish's mural *Old King Cole*, which was originally commissioned for The Knickerbocker, was installed above the bar at the St. Regis in 1932 once Prohibition ended. The 30-by-8-foot mural underwent an extensive cleaning in 2007—to the tune of $100,000—to restore this masterpiece to its former glory, its secret intact.

John Jacob Astor IV opened this Beaux-Arts hotel in 1904, just off Fifth Avenue. Astor was part of America's first wave of aristocratic families that rose to prominence during the Gilded Age, the name of which was taken from the title of Mark Twain's 1873 satire. Edith Wharton captured the upper class society of 1870s New York at the beginning of the

Gilded Age in her Pulitzer Prize–winning novel, *The Age of Innocence.* The hotel, considered the height of luxury at the time, was known for sumptuous parties attended by the rich and the powerful, the movers and shakers. Russian writer Maxim Gorky, a Marxist, had lunch in this lavish landmark in 1906. He told a *New York Times* reporter that "neither the Grand Dukes, nor even the Czar, have anything like this."

After Astor IV died aboard the *Titanic* in 1912 while trying to free his dog, Kitty, from the liner's kennel (after placing his young pregnant wife in a lifeboat), his son Vincent inherited the hotel. He later sold it to Benjamin Duke, who added two floors atop the hotel's roof. The two floors became the talk of town because of the lavish parties that occurred there, with such jazz greats as Count Basie and Duke Ellington entertaining. Vincent repurchased the property in 1935.

The King Cole Bar and the hotel play a titillating role in some writers' lives as well as in the plot of a spy novel. Founder of the prestigious Pen/Faulkner award, author Mary Lee Settle divulged in her memoir *Learning to Fly* that after a rooftop waltz with Prince Serge Obolensky, a key player in the Bloody Mary's arrival in the United States, she lost her virginity to him in a St. Regis room. John Cheever, who claimed that he was conceived at the St. Regis, drank many a martini looking up at King Cole. He had an easy walk home, for he lived around the corner.

In Ian Fleming's 1954 novel, *Live and Let Die*, famed spy James Bond arrives in New York to meet FBI and CIA agents at the St. Regis, where he takes a room. "At six twenty-five he went down to the King Cole Bar and chose a table near the entrance and against the wall," Fleming writes. Bond's contact arrives and orders medium-dry martinis for both of them. "The American gin, a much higher proof than English gin, tasted harsh to Bond. He reflected that he would have to be careful what he drank that evening."

Astor IV himself was quite a bibliophile. His personal library of some 3,000 books, which he ordered from Charles Scribner's Sons, a book publisher on Fifth Avenue several blocks away, included *The Adventures of Sherlock Holmes*, *Oliver Twist*, and *Alice's Adventures in Wonderland*. (Alas, the Scribner's bookstore closed in the eighties. Fortunately, the makeup store now in its place has maintained its beautiful bones.) The current owners have had his library digitized for hotel guests. A portion of his original collection has been on display behind glass at the hotel for more than a century.

Raise your glass to King Cole, the not-so-merry old soul in the mural, and cajole the bartender into revealing its somewhat irreverent secret.

RED SNAPPER: THE ORIGINAL BLOODY MARY

The Bloody Mary as we know it today is the creation of Fernand Petiot, the bartender who hailed from Harry's New York Bar in Paris. When he was hired to man the King Cole Bar in 1934, he introduced a spicier version of the cocktail, which he renamed "Red Snapper," to New York drinkers. The cocktail's original name, "Bloody Mary," was considered too offensive to hotel guests. He had made it at the request of Prince Serge Obolensky, a Russian who had a similar vodka drink in Paris. Obolensky was also the brother-in-law of Vincent Astor. The King Cole Bar offers five versions, plus Petiot's fabled recipe.

INGREDIENTS

2 ounces tomato juice

2 ounces vodka

½ teaspoon Worcestershire sauce

1 pinch salt

1 pinch cayenne pepper

1 dash lemon juice

DIRECTIONS

Place all ingredients in an ice-filled cocktail shaker. Shake well. Serve in a Delmonico glass.

The Red Snapper

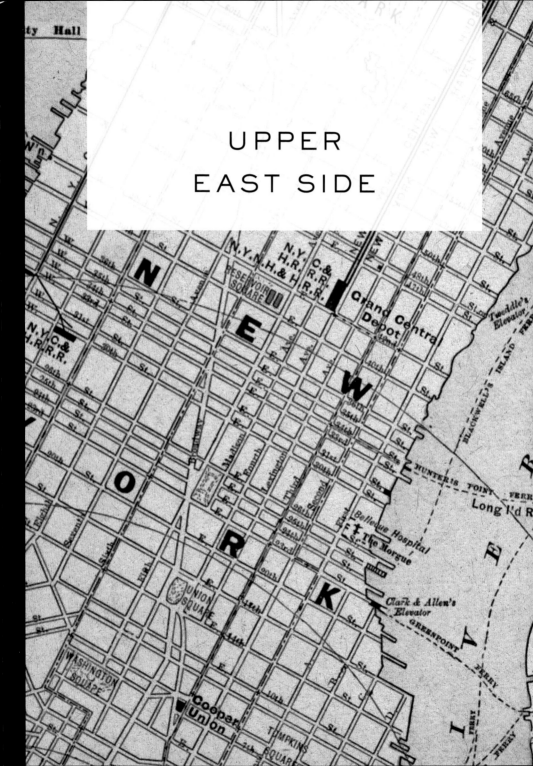

UPPER
EAST SIDE

The Upper East Side is where Holden Caulfield, the narrator of J. D. Salinger's *The Catcher in the Rye*, lives with his family. A century before this once-controversial novel was published in 1951, the families of the Gilded Age arrived—Fricks, Carnegies, Whitneys, Roosevelts, Rockefellers, and Vanderbilts. They built their estates in the area between Fifth Avenue and the East River from 59th Street to 96th Street. Edith Wharton lived in a townhouse on the corner of 57th Street and 5th Avenue, a perfect perch for her to write her fictionalized accounts of New York's high society. Since then, Millionaire's Row has been designated Museum Mile because of the number of museums along 5th Avenue and its side streets.

Other authors who have set their books in the UES are Truman Capote (*Breakfast at Tiffany's*), Avery Corman (*Kramer vs. Kramer*), Nora Ephron (*Heartburn*), Louise Fitzhugh (*Harriet the Spy*), and Tom Wolfe (*The Bonfire of the Vanities*). Authors Joan Didion, Jonathan Franzen, Caroline Kennedy, Jacqueline Kennedy Onassis, Malachi Brendan Martin, George Plimpton, and Gay Talese are either past or current residents.

Bemelmans Bar/ Hotel Carlyle

35 E. 76th Street (between Madison and Park avenues)
rosewoodhotels.com/en/the-carlyle-new-york
212-744-1600
Bar snacks and light meals: 5 to 11:30 p.m.
Entertainment (cover charge and beverage minimum):
Sunday and Monday, 5:30 to 8:30 p.m. and 9 p.m. to midnight;
Tuesday through Thursday, 5:30 to 8:30 p.m. and 9:30 p.m. to 12:30 a.m.;
Friday and Saturday, 5:30 to 8:30 p.m. and 9:30 p.m. to 1 a.m.

———

Ludwig Bemelmans may have been inspired to write his Madeline series while at Pete's Tavern, where he sketched the preliminary plot on the back of a menu in September 1938, but this bar provided him with a far more magnificent canvas: the walls.

Bemelmans, who was a prolific illustrator and writer for *The New Yorker*, *Vogue*, and *Town and Country*, was born in his family's hotel in Austria on April 27, 1898. After expulsion from several schools, the difficult teen was sent to work at an uncle's hotel in Tyrol, Austria, which is now in Italy. When his boss, the headwaiter, threatened to beat him with a heavy whip, Bemelmans warned that he would shoot him if he did. The waiter followed through on his threat, Bemelmans on his. The waiter nearly died from one shot to his abdomen. The police told his family that they had two options: reform school or America. With letters of introduction to several New York hotels, the 16-year-old boarded a ship. He landed a job as a busboy at the Ritz Carlton in Manhattan. He was fired for breaking too many dishes.

Bemelmans enlisted in the army during World War I. When he returned he wrote his first book about his experiences, *My War with the U.S.A.*, published in 1918. The writing, as ever, is marked by his quirkiness, sense of humor, and playfulness. Meanwhile, he continued to live in hotels. In 1935, he married Madeleine Freund (he deleted the second "e" because Madeline rhymed more easily). In 1939, *Madeline* was published. Its price was two dollars. He wrote six books in this series that has delighted children and adults alike, plus other children's books and books for adults—nearly 50 in all.

In one of his books about his travels, Bemelmans wrote that "his greatest inspiration is a low bank balance." Smart move for us all. He literally earned a place in cocktail history. He proposed that in exchange for 18 months' room and board at the elegant Carlyle he would paint a mural in the bar, which he completed in 1947.

The mural, which covers several walls and columns, depicts charming scenes in Central Park with his characteristically whimsical depictions of people, ice-skating elephants, picnicking rabbits, and Madeline and her fellow little orphans "in two straight lines." Bemelmans' drawings are a mix of sophistication and the childlike. In appreciation of his endeavor, the hotel named its bar after him. For a man who took his first breath in a hotel and spent a lifetime drawing on the backs of menus, tablecloths, and the inside covers of matchbooks, the honor is fitting. (The hotel, which opened in 1930, is named for the Scottish essayist Thomas Carlyle.)

The gold-toned background of the mural blends with the 24-karat gold-leaf-covered ceiling and complements the Art Deco style of the bar's leather banquettes and nickel-trimmed black glass tabletops. On each table sits a small lamp with shades that feature drawings of New York City sights inspired by Bemelmans's illustrations. The small tables in the rest of the room are placed close together and surround the sleek ebony grand piano. Every night, the bar features live music. Cyndi Lauper, Bono, Liza Minnelli, and Billy Joel have performed at the spur of the moment when they've stopped in for a drink.

The bar feels like being steeped in the pages of one of Bemelmans's children's books. This intimate space, with its warm lighting and cool vibe, is a perfect place to ponder Madeline's adventures while nursing a cocktail and soaking in the bar's glamour. The bar attracts authors, editors, and publishers who come for their five o'clock cocktail. In years past, Truman Capote would meet Jacqueline Kennedy for drinks at the bar. (Her second husband, Aristotle Onassis, commissioned Bemelmans to paint a mural for the children's dining room on his yacht.) Capote often suggested meeting reporters there for his interviews. However, the bar is not for adults only. In November and December, Saturdays are reserved for "Madeline Tea," with two seatings, mid-morning and 12:30 p.m., for children.

J. Courtney Sullivan, however, didn't go to the teas. When she was a little girl, her grandfather took her to Bemelmans whenever they visited New York City. "I'd wear a frilly party dress and Mary Janes and sip a Shirley Temple as a jazz trio played," the Massachusetts native says. In

2003, she moved to New York and lived on ramen noodles to write for a woman's magazine and later *The New York Times*. She could not afford a cocktail at Bemelmans, but every so often, a high school friend who worked at an investment firm would treat her to an evening of jazz and a cocktail. "To me the place embodies a New York that only exists in movies," says Sullivan, now a best-selling novelist. "I still love arriving there, setting foot in that room, so full of memories."

THE OLD CUBAN

Recipe courtesy of Bemelmans Bar

Ludwig Bemelmans traveled often. In his book *The Donkey Inside*, he recounts his adventures in Ecuador. The book is out of print, but Bemelmans first wrote about his Ecuador trip for *The New Yorker*, and the piece can be found on the magazine's website. He and his wife, Madeleine, were among the passengers on the maiden voyage of the *Queen Elizabeth I* to New York in 1940. (The ship had been painted battleship grey for this secret trip, dodging German U-boats as it traversed the Atlantic during World War II. Immediately after, she began transporting troops. After the war ended, she resumed life as an ocean liner.)

On one of his trips, the Bemelmans family rendezvoused with Ernest Hemingway and Dorothy Parker in Paris. Bemelmans's letters to Hemingway are archived with the rest of Hemingway's papers in the John F. Kennedy Presidential Library. The family friendship extended to another generation. Hemingway's grandson Edward shares an art studio with John Bemelmans Marciano in Brooklyn. The two are illustrators and writers.

Given that Hemingway lived in Cuba for 20 years, you could commemorate Ludwig and Papa's family ties and creativity with an Old Cuban, one of the bar's most popular drinks. When mixologist Audrey Saunders created this cocktail in a New York bar in 2002, it became a contemporary classic.

Hemingway's *The Old Man and the Sea* pairs well with this cocktail, or indulge your inner child and pull out that tattered copy of *Madeline*.

INGREDIENTS

2 ounces Bacardi Ocho
2 ounces fresh lime juice

1½ ounces simple syrup

2 dashes Angostura bitters

Fresh mint sprigs

1 splash of Canard-Duchêne Champagne

DIRECTIONS

To a mixing glass, add the simple syrup, lime juice, and a mint sprig. Muddle gently. Fill with ice. Add the rum, followed by the bitters. Shake vigorously. Strain into a chilled martini glass. Top with the champagne. Garnish with a mint sprig.

The Old Cuban

Elaine's

APPETIZERS

Grilled Shrimp on Garlic Toast	15.75
Clams on the Half Shell	12.75
Calamari Fritti	14.75
Smoked Scottish Salmon	16.75
Antipasto (for two)	16.75
Artichoke Vinaigrette	12.75
Steamed Mussels	15.75
Ligurian Anchovies with Roasted Red Peppers	15.75

Melon & Prosciutto San Daniele	15.75
Beef Carpaccio with Arugula	16.75
Baked Clams Oreganato	12.75
Zucchini Fritti	10.75
Shrimp Cocktail	15.75
Prosciutto, Mozzerella Di Buffala	16.75
Roasted Peppers	

SALADS

House Salad	10.75
Spinach Salad	14.75
Tri-Color Salad	12.75
Caesar Salad	12.75
Tomato and Vidalia Onion with Goat Cheese	14.75

PESCE

Salmon Paillard with Chopped Salad	27.75
Sauteed Brook Trout Almandine	25.75
Shrimp Fra Diavolo	29.75
Zuppa Di Pesce	3?

PASTA

Spaghetti Bolognese	22.75
Linguini Primavera	21.75
Linguini with Clam Sauce	24.75
Spaghetti Squash Vegetable Marinara	21.75
Spaghetti with Anchovies & Capers	21.75
Tortelloni with Peas & Prosciutto	24.75
Capellini with Wild Mushrooms and Sage Butter	23.75

CARNE

Veal Scallopini Piccata	30.75
Veal Marsala with Wild Mushrooms	31.75
Veal Saltimbocca	32.75
Broiled Sirloin Steak	43.75
Broiled Veal Chop	43.75
Veal Milanese & Tri-Color Salad	32.75
Sauteed Calf's Liver Veneziano	27.75
Free-Range Chicken Limone	26.75
Chicken Paillard with Salad	26.75
Hamburger with French Fries	15.75

VEGETABLES

Broccoli Di Rape	12.75
Potato Fritti	9.75
Sauteed Broccoli or Spinach	12.75

Room Available for Private Parties

Elaine's

(see The Writing Room)

1703 2nd Avenue
Closed.

In 1979, when the then unknown and, in his words, "overconfident
youthful brash" Jay McInerney arrived in Manhattan, the aspiring writer
yearned to be among the literary lions who packed the tables and bar
nightly at Elaine's: Hunter S. Thompson, Nora Ephron, Joan Didion,
and Pete Hamill, to name a few. The year before, Billy Joel had immor-
talized the watering hole in his song "Big Shot." Within a few years,
McInerney had written a best-seller, *Bright Lights, Big City*, became
part of a literary "brat pack" (other members were Bret Easton Ellis and
Tama Janowitz), and gained notoriety for his cocaine-fueled partying.
McInerney also became One of Them, a habitué of Elaine's.

The writers weren't there for the Italian food, which one restaurant
critic deemed "edible," the chicken livers and kidneys akin to "damp
cardboard." No, the literati came for the club-like atmosphere, for the
camaraderie, for the schmoozing, for the booze, and for Elaine herself.

A *Vanity Fair* interviewer told her, "You have a soft spot for writers." Elaine replied, "Poor bastards, I like their minds." She added,

"Writers have never come to my place to talk about literature. They come to escape writing." Elaine's raucous mob was a respite from a day spent alone at a typewriter.

In the late 1950s, Elaine Kaufman, a lifelong New Yorker, worked at a Greenwich Village restaurant called Portofino's, which attracted struggling writers and artists with its cheap Italian food. She helped the owner, with whom she became romantically involved, run the place. After they broke up, Elaine, along with business partner and playwright Jack Richardson, bought an Austrian-Hungarian restaurant for $10,000 in the Yorkville section of the Upper East Side in 1963. Yorkville lacked any of the Village's bohemian culture.

Elaine, who had started to read at age 4 and claimed she read the entire contents of a used book store where she once worked, envisioned a "saloon salon" for the literati. Richardson vowed to lure his writer friends and suggested they fill the restaurant with large tables so that patrons could visit one other. Some of her old customers, including the painters Helen Frankenthaler and Robert Motherwell, Woody Allen, and newspaper gossip columnist Dorothy Kilgallen, followed her uptown. Within a year, struggling as well as established writers started coming regularly, among them Joseph Heller, William Styron, Norman Mailer, George Plimpton, Tom Wolfe, and Gay Talese. They brought writers with them, who in turn brought other writer friends. Other personalities, also enamored of writers, followed. After eight years, Elaine bought her partner out. And as the writers became successes, they remained loyal to their oasis.

The Italian meals didn't cost much, and if you were a writer who was hard up for cash, Elaine wouldn't make you pay. During a newspaper strike, broke reporters and columnists drank on tabs. Winston Groom paid up a bar tab of several thousand dollars when the movie rights to his novel *Forrest Gump* were sold.

From the beginning, the place was purely Elaine's. She had rummaged through antique and junk shops to furnish and decorate her new saloon, providing it with an eclectic and quirky air. A vintage black metal cash register was parked behind the bar. A large papier-mâché Christmas carousel horse occupied a front window. By the entrance sat a neon-lit jukebox. The pendant lights were rumored to be from a funeral home. The vinyl canopy and awnings over the sidewalk, as well as the awning above the 25-foot mahogany bar, were rain-slicker yellow. Patrons were greeted by sign bearing a Samuel Johnson quotation: "There is no private house in which people can enjoy themselves so well as at a capital tavern."

Elaine did not ignore the walls. The lower portion above the chair railings featured sepia-toned murals of scenes that suggested rural Italy. In addition to antlers and deer heads, authentic art nouveau French posters and paintings by Frankenthaler were placed on the walls.

Over time, the dark walls became an homage to her regulars. As the writers published *New York Times* best-sellers, the covers were framed— several hundred by the time Elaine's closed—and joined the rest of the bric-a-brac. Shelves held piles of signed first editions. Blown-up prints of book covers and magazine covers were propped up around them. Tacked up wherever a bit of real estate allowed were framed photos of writers, movie stars, singers, editors, directors, agents, pro athletes, publicists, and other New York insiders enjoying the nightly cocktail party that was Elaine's. Andy Warhol, David Hockney, and other artist patrons also contributed their work to this mix. Movie posters, signed, also went up. The decor was haphazard. Who sat where, however, was not.

Elaine, with her big round eyeglasses, her earrings commemorating a New York Yankees World Series win, and her custom-made colorful dresses, was renowned as an imperious restaurateur. While big-hearted, she could be cranky, salty, unfriendly, and abrasive, and she had punched a customer or two in her lifetime. Each evening until about 2 a.m.—or a little earlier in her later years—the grand hostess oversaw the smoke-filled, rowdy scene, often delivering the checks to each table herself. Sometimes, she perched herself on the first oak stool along the bar to keep an eye on things, ensuring that people were seated according to her pecking order.

A row of round tables covered with blue-and-white checkered tablecloths hugged the long wall opposite the packed bar. These seats were known as "The Line." Elaine chose which members of her flock sat at the tables. Table 1 was reserved for VIPs. Table 4 belonged to Elaine and her closest regulars, such as Bruce Jay Friedman and William Styron. For 10 years, Woody Allen occupied Table 8 nightly, often alone, eating and ignoring the revelers. No one dared approach him to chat. (One night, Elaine told a customer looking for the men's room, "Make a right at Woody Allen.)

On any given night, every table along The Line was filled with literary boldfacers, mostly men, because Elaine favored them. George Plimpton and Norman Mailer holding forth over Scotch. Tom Wolfe telling tales in his signature white suit. McInerney, with his latest fashion-model girlfriend at his side, sipping chianti. Pete Hamill with his girlfriend, Shirley MacLaine, taking seats among them, having just quaffed a few at the Lion's Head (see page 45) in the Village. Hamill's journalist kid brother, Denis, had a book party there in 1980 for his first novel, *Stomping Ground*. Elaine would take new writers from table to table to make the introductions.

And if Elaine didn't like you? She relegated you to the back room, nicknamed Siberia by her regulars, with the nobodies, the wannabes, and the lookers-on.

During the course of an evening, writers table-hopped, cigarette butts accumulated in glass ashtrays imprinted in yellow with "Elaine's WE'RE ALWAYS TOGETHER," and the crowd grew drunker, larger, and louder. People played backgammon and card games. News reporters arrived after making their last deadline.

Occasionally, this watering hole had provided gossip-columnist fodder beyond who was seen there on a given night. Once, Elaine was arrested and jailed overnight for an altercation with one customer. On another occasion, Elaine unwittingly attempted to introduce one of her regulars, Mario Puzo, author of *The Godfather*, to Frank Sinatra, who was displeased with Puzo's portrayal of Italians and the mafia. Sinatra refused to shake hands. Woody Allen first met Mia Farrow there. When Jacqueline Kennedy started dating Greek shipping magnate Aristotle Onassis, Elaine seated them at the more secluded Table 10. Mailer fired off an angry letter to Elaine accusing her of not liking his latest girlfriend. Elaine scrawled "boring, boring, boring" on the missive and mailed it back to him. But mostly, patrons could imbibe and make a fool of themselves and no one cared.

The nightspot took a hit during the 2008 economic downturn, and business declined. Two years later, Kaufman died from complications of emphysema at age 81. She left the restaurant to her manager, Diane Becker. Without Elaine, who was named a Living Landmark by the New York Landmarks Conservancy in 2003, business slowed even more, and Becker opted to end the 48-year-long cocktail party.

After a goodbye party attended by Elaine's tribe of writers, politicians, TV personalities, movie stars, and anyone else who was part of the inner circle, the restaurant had its last call on May 26, 2011. The restaurant's and her home's contents were auctioned. Table 1 and four cafe chairs sold for $8,750, the antique cash register and the carousel horse brought in $4,062 each, and four oak bar stools went for $1,250. Becker donated the sign with its cursive "Elaine's," which had welcomed so many writers, to the New-York Historical Society.

Elaine's had cameos in at least two movies: a dinner scene in *Diary of a Mad Housewife* and the opening scene of *Manhattan*.

After her death, a group of writers founded the Table 4 Foundation, which annually awards grants to five promising writers, in Elaine's honor.

The Writing Room, a bistro with literary ambience, has taken its place.

ADDITIONAL WRITERS AND OTHER LITERATI FOR WHOM ELAINE'S WAS LIKE A SECOND HOME:

Simone de Beauvoir

Truman Capote

Robert Caro

Mary Higgins Clark

Frank Conroy

Clay Felker

David Halberstam

Joseph Heller

Lewis Lapham

Peter Maas

Aleksandr Solzhenitsyn

NEGRONI

Jay McInerney's tastes have shifted from hard liquor and cocaine to fine wines, but when it comes to cocktails, he's a martini man. In the late 1990s, he ventured into the world of wine writing. "My ambition to be a novelist and my interest in wine were both inspired by Hemingway's *The Sun Also Rises*," he wrote. "I wanted to write like Hemingway and drink like Jake Barnes." He told a *Wall Street Journal* reporter in 2009, "I gave up cocktails for a while, and I had to come back to them. They're just so much fun. Sometimes you have to get a quick infusion of alcohol in order to face the night."

The Negroni was conceived by a bartender at a cafe in Florence, Italy in 1919 or thereabouts. Like so many cocktail backstories, that bar tale comes with a shot of doubt.

INGREDIENTS

1 ounce gin
1 ounce Campari
1 ounce sweet vermouth
Orange twist

DIRECTIONS

Stir ingredients in a mixing glass filled with ice. Strain into a chilled cocktail glass or serve in an ice-filled old-fashioned glass. Garnish with orange twist.

The Writing Room

1703 2nd Avenue (at 88th Street)
thewritingroomnyc.com
212-335-0075
Monday: 4 to 10:30 p.m.
Tuesday through Thursday: 11:45 a.m. to 10:30 p.m.
Friday: 11:45 a.m. to 11:30 p.m.
Saturday: 11 a.m. to 11:30 p.m.
Sunday: 11 a.m. to 10 p.m.

When restaurateurs Michael and Susy Glick took over the former Elaine's, they chose to honor its literary roots and then go a little further. The brick walls are original, but the layout was switched. The dining room is now to the left of the entrance, the bar to the right. The to-the-studs renovation entailed enclosing the outdoor space behind Elaine's. From the zinc-wrapped bar to the reclaimed wood floors, The Writing Room has a vintage feel. The new back room, called "The Study," is lined with built-in bookcases filled with books, many from the owner's father's personal library. "You can sit and read the books if you want to," says general manager Isabel Costa-Chan. Manual typewriters occupy a center shelf.

The walls of the main dining room are covered with black-and-white photos taken at Elaine's as well as additional pictures of illustrious

authors such as F. Scott Fitzgerald, who never set foot in this building. Some of Elaine's patrons have returned. The Italian-influenced food is better. Several cocktails have names with a literary twist: "The Last Word," "Smith & Corona," and "Sonnet XVIII." The latter includes gin, grapefruit juice, honey, and lime—it tastes like a summer's day. Shakespeare would be pleased.

A women's book club holds their meetings amid these bookish surroundings. People don't think twice about reading a book at the bar.

SMITH & CORONA*

Recipe courtesy of The Writing Room

Oh, for the love of the clackety sound of the keys on a typewriter and the books produced on them! Novelist Tayari Jones's fascination with typewriters began during her childhood in Atlanta. "I imagined myself writing books one day, and I would raise a mighty racket, without once glancing at my hands," she says. She collects typewriters and writes the early drafts of her novels on them. "The manual typewriter is totally unconnected from the internet. No distractions," she says. When Jones calls it quits after a day of writing, she opts for a spirit-forward cocktail, such as a classic martini.

Writers back in the day were partial to particular makes of typewriters. Jones loves manual typewriters from the thirties and forties. "Scores of little touches—for example, glossy finish, fetching carrying case, and the little crook for your finger on the return carriage lever. So elegant!" she says.

Smith-Corona typewriters were the machines of choice for so many authors—and still are. Donald Barthelme, Raymond Carver, Julio Cortàzar, Walter Cronkite, E. E. Cummings, Isak Dinesen, Dr. Seuss (a.k.a. Theodore Geisel), T. S. Eliot, M. F. K. Fisher, Nikki Giovanni, Joseph Heller, George S. Kaufman, Ring Lardner, David Mamet, Arthur Miller, Dorothy Parker, and David Foster Wallace relied on these beauties to make their words flow.

Robert Caro composes his massive books on a Smith-Corona Electra. He keeps nine spares for parts and stockpiles typewriter ribbons. Truman Capote typed his books on an earlier model in the Electra series, as did William Styron.

Aldous Huxley, Sinclair Lewis, and Ernest Hemingway used the nifty Corona 3. This

---

*Name as it appears on the menu. The typewriter company was known as "Smith-Corona."

The Smith & Corona

lightweight, portable typewriter had a unique feature: a carriage and ribbon spools that folded over the glass-coated keys to make it even more compact. An optional tripod screwed into the bottom, so that a war correspondent could stand and type his stories on the front. Hemingway carried this gem to Cuba, Spain, Germany, France, and Switzerland. His first novel, *The Sun Also Rises*, was tapped out on this typewriter, which is displayed at the Museo Ernest Hemingway in Cuba.

In a 1918 letter to his father, Hemingway wrote, "To take a story over the phone and get everything exact, see it all in your mind's eye, rush over to a typewriter and write it a page at a time while ten other typewriters are going and the boss is hollering at someone and a boy snatches the page from our machine as fast as you write them. How long would a lot of people I know last at that before going wild?"

This spicy cocktail would definitely take the edge off that scene.

INGREDIENTS

2 ounces bell-pepper-infused tequila

½ ounce yellow chartreuse

½ ounce honey

¾ ounce fresh lime juice

Ancho-sea-salt mix for glass rim

DIRECTIONS

Pour a thin layer of ancho-salt mix on a plate. Dampen edge of a highball glass with water. Combine all ingredients in an ice-filled cocktail shaker. Place the ancho-sea salt on a plate. Press upside-down glass into the salt to coat the rim. Strain over ice in the ancho-sea-salt rimmed glass.

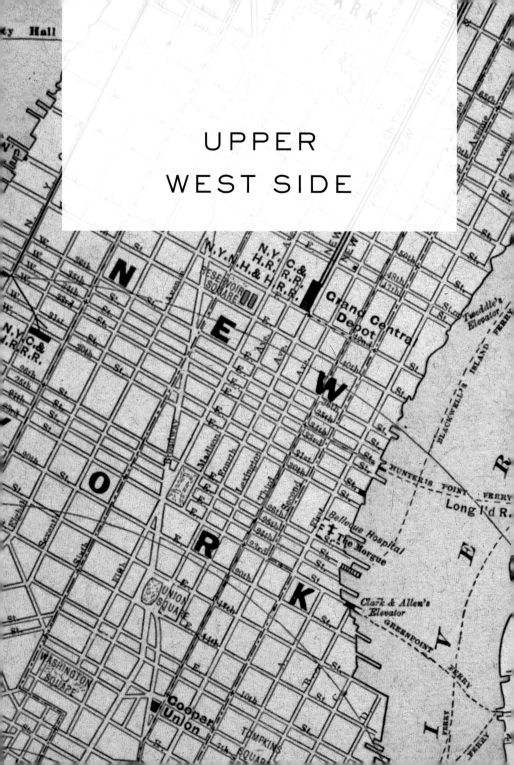

UPPER
WEST SIDE

The Upper West Side, which extends from West 59th Street and Central Park South to West 125th Street, includes Morningside Heights to the north. The Hudson River forms a boundary on the west, with Central Park and Morningside Park to the east.

The Upper West Side was, and remains, an enclave to quite a number of the literati: Dorothy Parker, Nora Ephron, Charles Henri Ford, Carson McCullers, Eugene O'Neill, Tennessee Williams, Peter Straub, Harlan Coben, and Tina Fey. In 1844, Edgar Allan Poe and his wife, Virginia, took up residence in a farmhouse near West 84th Street and Broadway, when the area was still rural. Poe wrote "The Raven" while residing there. Joan Didion recounted the death of her husband, John Gregory Dunne, in their UWS apartment and her subsequent grieving in *The Year of Magical Thinking*. The Upper West Side also served as the setting or had a cameo role in such books as *The Catcher in the Rye*, *The Great Gatsby*, *Rosemary's Baby*, *The New Yorkers*, *Sister Carrie*, *Time and Again*, and *Seize the Day*.

The Dead Poet

450 Amsterdam Avenue (between 81st and 82nd streets)
212-595-5670
thedeadpoet.com
Daily: 12 p.m. to 4 a.m.

The Dead Poet was opened by Andrew Dworkin, a former English teacher, in 2000. "The literary theme evolved from what he knew as an English teacher," says Kevin Cole, who was the bar's general manager for eight years until he bought the place in 2015. Its mahogany paneling is covered with black-and-white portraits of famed poets and writers and quotations from prose and poetry. Cole keeps a stock of used books for customers to read while there or to borrow. This Irish bar, with its academic atmosphere meets pub, is on the same block as the New York Public Library's St. Agnes branch.

Upper West Side residents and college students stop by for its literary-inspired cocktails, 60-plus varieties of whiskey, and its perfect pour of a pint of Guinness served with a shamrock. "People come here to sit and scribble in their notebooks," Cole says. During the summer, the crowds and actors from Shakespeare in the Park, a free offering of Shakespeare's plays by the Public Theater in Central Park, drop in after the performance. For food, the owner partners with a bar across the street, which has a kitchen and delivers the food.

The bar, as narrow as an old railroad car, is located a mere three blocks from where Dorothy Parker attended grade school on West 79th Street, between Amsterdam and Columbus avenues. On the cocktail menu, you'll find a drink named for Dottie as well as ones for J. D. Salinger, Ernest Hemingway, Tennessee Williams, Pablo Neruda, Robert Burns, Frank McCourt, and Edgar Allen Poe. The Tempest, Tell-Tale Heart, Scarlet Letter, and Legend of Sleepy Hollow cocktails pay homage to literature.

Customers who share a birthday with a deceased poet or author may have a drink on the house on that day.

WALT WHITMAN

Recipe courtesy of The Dead Poet

This version of a Long Island Iced Tea honors Walt Whitman, who was born in 1819 in the West Hills hamlet of Huntington, Long Island.

INGREDIENTS

½ ounce citrus vodka

½ ounce gin

½ ounce coconut rum

½ ounce orange liqueur

Sour mix

Orange juice

Luxardo cherry

Lemon

DIRECTIONS

Combine liquors in an ice-filled cocktail shaker. Shake. Pour into an ice-filled collins glass. Top with sour mix and a splash of orange juice. Garnish with cherry and lemon slice.

The Langston Hughes

LANGSTON HUGHES

Recipe courtesy of The Dead Poet

The bar renamed the Sidecar, a jazz-era cocktail, after Langston Hughes, whose own writing is influenced by jazz. Hughes attended Columbia University for a year.

INGREDIENTS

2 ounces Hine cognac

¾ ounce orange-flavored liqueur

½ ounce fresh lemon juice

½ ounce simple syrup

Flamed lemon peel for garnish

DIRECTIONS

Combine all ingredients in a cocktail shaker filled with ice. Shake and strain into a chilled martini glass. Garnish with lemon peel.

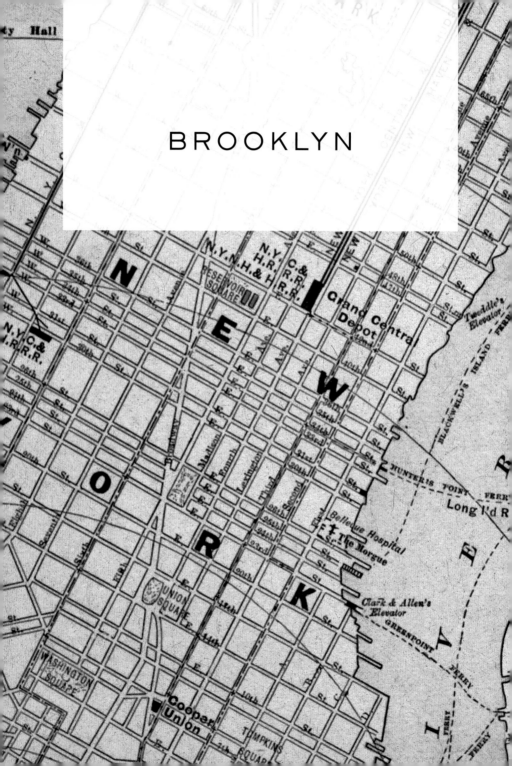

BROOKLYN

Brooklyn has become a magnet for bookish types in recent decades. Its rents are somewhat more affordable than those of that literary mecca across the East River. That's not to say that Brooklyn never had a literary past. Walt Whitman, whose formative years were spent there, wrote for several Brooklyn newspapers before the Civil War. Brooklyn also has been home to Carson McCullers, Arthur Miller, Richard Wright, Truman Capote, Hart Crane, Marianne Moore, and W. H. Auden. Norman Mailer threw his legendary, boisterous soirees in his Brooklyn Heights digs. Pete Hamill, who grew up a block away from Prospect Park, first got drunk here while working in the Brooklyn Navy Yard. He recalls his childhood and early writing career in his gritty memoir, *A Drinking Life*.

More recently, a stellar cast of writers has come to call the borough home: Katie Roiphe, Jonathan Lethem, Jennifer Egan, Kurt Anderson, Emily St. John Mandel, Amitav Ghosh, Susan Choi, Touré, Paul Auster, Nicole Krauss, Elissa Schappell, and Rick Moody.

In 2012, when journalist turned-screenwriter-Michael Maren wanted to film a coffee shop scene for his movie *A Short History of Decay*, he chose Kos Kaffe in Park Slope, a second office for many Brooklyn writers. He enlisted three dozen published authors as extras to sit at the tables, laptops open. His direction: Give a "you don't belong here" stare as the film's protagonist, a struggling writer—naturally—slinks out. A *New York Times* reporter called it a "very meta Brooklyn literary moment . . . the most impressive mass literary cameo in recent film history."

On Brooklyn's resurgent literary community and in praise of the Brooklyn-based literary magazine *n+1*, Malcolm Gladwell noted, "Intelligent thought is not dead in New York. It has simply moved to Brooklyn."

Franklin Park

618 St. John's Place (between Franklin and Classon avenues)
franklinparkbrooklyn.com
franklinparkreadingseries.tumblr.com
718-230-0293 (Dutch Boy Burger, the restaurant attached to the bar)
Weekdays: 3 p.m. to 4 a.m.
Weekends: 1 p.m. to 4 a.m.
See website for reading series dates

Ambling around Crown Heights, Matthew Roff and Anatoly Dubinsky happened on a dilapidated garage in 2007 and envisioned a bar and outdoor beer garden. Franklin Park, with its urban vintage ambience, opened the following year. The pair are part of a recent wave of people making Brooklyn the "it" borough. As recently as the nineties, Crown Heights was a rough place, filled with racial tension and abandoned buildings. In the late nineteenth century, this section of Brooklyn featured "Millionaire's Row," several blocks lined with mansions. Since its opening, Franklin Park has become a neighborhood mainstay with its rotating selection of craft brews on draft and, since 2009, an award-winning reading series on the second Monday of every month.

Freelance writer Penina Roth, who has lived in Crown Heights for two-plus decades, wrote a *New York Times* piece about the new bar in 2008. Noting the neighborhood's ethnic diversity and the twentysomethings settling in, Roth reported that Ari Kirschenbaum, the rabbi from

the synagogue opposite the bar, has held Hasidic philosophy classes at this bar. After attending author readings at other bars, she approached Franklin Park's owners about holding a book series. "Everyone in Crown Heights is very literary," she says. "The [bar's] beer garden is always filled with people reading books."

In March 2009, she hosted the first reading. Word spread. *Time Out* called it a "bookworm's dream dinner party." And the series, to Roth's surprise, took off. "It feeds on itself," says Rachel Cantor, who read to a packed house when her novel *Good on Paper* was published in 2016. (Cantor also had readings for her novel at KGB and Pete's Candy Store.)

Franklin Park, as you can see, didn't have to go far to recruit writers for its reading series, although Roth draws in novelists, poets, and other raconteurs from locales as far away as Nigeria, Haiti, and China. On a typical reading night, two or more writers are featured in the lineup. Roth tries to book at least one celebrity headliner, say, Colson Whitehead or Edwidge Danticat. A night might have a theme, such as readings by memoirists, contributors to a literary journal, women pushing lit boundaries, short story writers, or veterans of the wars in Iraq and Afghanistan.

The writers stand on a small raised platform in a corner of the bar and read from their work to a packed house. Sometimes, the crowd spills out into the outdoor beer garden. Fortunately, the writer uses a microphone so that all can hear. While the bar offers a craft beer special to accompany the event, listening to readings by top-notch writers is why people are there.

Readings have featured Julia Fierro, Amy Hempel, Alexander Chee, Dani Shapiro, Stanley Crouch, Jami Attenberg, Amy Brill, Colson Whitehead, Jennifer Gilmore, Shalom Auslander, and Tayari Jones. People working in the book world and magazine industry attend because they can't get enough of great writing.

The bar holds joint events with the Brooklyn Book Festival in October and partners for special events with PEN American Center. This venue is also the site of many book launch parties.

BROOKLYN EAGLE

Franklin Park does serve cocktails, but mainly it offers a wide selection of craft brews on tap and in bottles/cans. That's no reason not to recognize Brooklyn's own cocktail, which gives a nod to the newspaper at which Walt Whitman was an editor.

INGREDIENTS

2 ounces bourbon

1 ounce triple sec

½ ounce sweet vermouth

1 ounce fresh lime juice

DIRECTIONS

Combine all ingredients with cracked ice in a cocktail shaker. Shake well and strain into a chilled cocktail glass.

The Shanty/ New York Distilling Company

79 Richardson Street (between Leonard and Lorimer streets)
nydistilling.com
718-412-0874
Monday: 6 p.m. to 12 a.m.
Tuesday through Thursday: 6 p.m. to 2 a.m.
Friday: 5 p.m. to 2 a.m.
Saturday and Sunday: 2 p.m. to 12 a.m.
Distillery tours (free): Saturdays, 2:30, 3:30, and 5 p.m.
Dog (Sun)day afternoons: Sundays, 2 to 6 p.m.;
distillery doors open for cocktails and dog owners

———————

A Brooklyn boutique distillery that makes Dorothy Parker Gin? What's not to like? The New York Distilling Company, along with its bar, The Shanty, is a mere youngster building its literary reputation. Located in a former rag factory in the Williamsburg section of Brooklyn, the building,

with its corrugated metal and brick walls, seems like an unlikely setting
for this enterprise from the outside.

The craft distillery and its bar opened their doors in December
2011. The building is divided into two cavernous rooms. A wall of clear
glass windows separates the rooms. In one, stacks of wooden barrels
lie on their sides, three barrels high, on shelving. They contain three
kinds of gin and two types of rye whiskey. In this room, which smells of
liquor, they also mix, distill, bottle, and ship the company's five products.
Adjacent to the barrels sits an array of copper stills and stainless steel
tanks—some twice the height of an average adult—with pipes extending
upward and around the periphery of the room.

The full-service bar occupies the other room. The overall look, taste-
ful urban industrial, fits the building's factory past. Old-school metal

and wood lab stools surround the bar. The pendant lights are made of dark, square steel tubes with blond wooden tops carved to look like bottles of liquor. Open seven days a week, the bartender will mix a patron's must-have cocktail. They stock liquor brands other than their own.

Dorothy Parker Gin, an American gin, is made with nontraditional botanicals, namely hibiscus and elderberries. To that mix, they add citrus and the traditional botanical found in gin, juniper, says head distiller Bill Potter. Potter's father, Tom, is a co-founder. Allen Katz, a nationally known authority on spirits and cocktails and part of this distillery's team, suggested they name their spirits after prominent New Yorkers. When a fresh batch of gin is ready, they test it by making three classics: a gin and tonic, a gin sour, and a martini.

Another reason for the Dorothy Parker homage was that she frequented speakeasies, where gin was popular. (Parker's biographer Marion Meade writes that the writer preferred Scotch because gin made her "miserably sick.") Bill points out that Prohibition speakeasies had no qualms with having women patrons. "It became socially acceptable for a woman to drink in a speakeasy when it was

New York Distilling Company makes gin named for Dorothy Parker.

illegal," he says. Women meant more customers and, in turn, more revenue. In the 1700s, a number of distilleries operated in Brooklyn. Some 50,000 illegal stills in Brooklyn supplied the speaks all over.

In addition to distillery tours, the bar has served as a venue for the Dorothy Parker Society's gatherings—"a raucous group," Potter says. In December 2015, the entire bar and distillery space served as the stage for a production of *Macbeth*. The audience sipped Scotch, required drinking while watching the Scottish general. The after-theater cocktails were Macbeth-themed *sans* eye of newt. The theater company, Masterfool, performed *A Midsummer Night's Dream* several months before in the same venue.

THE ACERBIC
MRS. PARKER

Recipe courtesy of New York Distilling Company

So many adjectives have been deployed to describe Dorothy Parker's wit and writing. In legendary mixologist Allen Katz's book, Dottie deserves more than one eponymous cocktail. (See Blue Room/Algonquin entry for his other Parker-inspired recipe.) This cocktail packs a citrusy punch. The hibiscus syrup amplifies the hibiscus botanicals in the gin.

INGREDIENTS

2 ounces Dorothy Parker Gin

½ ounce fresh lemon juice

½ ounce hibiscus syrup

¾ ounce orange liqueur

DIRECTIONS

Shake ingredients in an ice-filled shaker. Strain into a collins glass filled with fresh ice. Top with club soda and garnish with a lemon wheel.

Concerts, events, and readings are the draw at Pete's.

Pete's Candy Store

708 Lorimer Street
petescandystore.com
718-302-3770
Sunday: 4 p.m. to 2 a.m.
Monday through Wednesday: 5 p.m. to 2 a.m.
Thursday: 5 p.m. to 4 a.m.
Friday and Saturday: 4 p.m. to 4 a.m.
See events calendar for readings

Around the corner from The Shanty/New York Distilling Company, Pete's Candy Store looks like a storefront. In fact, the bar was a general store called Funzi's in the 1920s. Five decades later, the general store having gradually evolved into a greasy-spoon diner with poker tables in back, Pete Caruso took over. In 1999, the current owners envisioned a bar, its layout comparable to a railroad apartment, with live entertainment.

The back alcove, where poker tables were once hidden, has a stage. Every other Thursday, the bar hosts Pete's Reading Series. Authors who have taken the stage include such luminaries as Jonathan Ames, Thomas Beller, Chloe Caldwell, Tobias Carroll, Lan Samantha Chang, Jennifer Egan, Hari Kunzru, Caroline Leavitt, David Lehman, Sam Lipsyte, Colum McCann, Francine Prose, Saïd Sayrafiezadeh, Gary Shteyngart, Anna Solomon, Hannah Tinti, Colm Tóibín, and Justin Torres. According to Shteyngart, Pete's is "the most intimate reading space in Brooklyn. Think of a fine pre-war dining car with an endless supply of booze."

On the second Friday of each month, Pete's Big Salmon, their popular poetry reading series, is held. Lisa Andrews, Tom Capelonga, Lawrence Kaplan, Quraysh Ali Lansana, Debora Lidov, Syreeta McFadden, Elizabeth Metzger, Stephen S. Mills, Tanya Olson, Camille Rankine, Danniel Schoonebeek, Nicole Sealey, Julie Marie Wade, and Matthew Yeager have all given readings of their work.

For emerging and published writers, Pete's added a Prose Bowl in 2015. The Bowl's co-founder, Christopher Green, a Midwest transplant, attended an open-mic poetry night and wondered why there weren't any such competitions for fiction writers. Over whiskey, Green and John Hague plotted out their idea and approached Pete's owner.

On the third Tuesday of each month, four writers picked at random from a hat participate in an open-mic showdown. The supportive audience consists of writers and bibliophiles. Three judges, Green, Hague, and a published author, listen to each writer's five-minute story of about 900 words and provide supportive yet clever reviews. Imagine a kinder, gentler *American Idol*, but for prose. Two finalists go on to the lightning round, during which they read a tweet-length short story. The winner, chosen by audience applause, gets a free drink of his or her choice. The evenings make for lively entertainment.

All past champions may compete at an annual event, held at the Kraine Theater under the KGB Bar. *ProseCast*, the series podcast, is available for free.

Boozy slushies, beer, cocktails, and sandwiches are on the menu.

BLACK RUSSIAN

Best-selling novelist Caroline Leavitt read from her 10th novel, *Cruel Beautiful World*, as part of Pete's Reading Series in the fall of 2016.

Leavitt has been drinking Black Russians since her college days. "When I got to college, I wanted to feel more adult, and I thought that writers were supposed to have bad habits, like drinking or cigarettes," she says. Because she has asthma, smoking was ruled off the table. Alcohol, then, would be her writerly vice. One afternoon, she went to a bar, notebook in hand, and ordered a Black Russian. The name appealed to her because her grandparents came from Russia. Plus, she loves coffee and chocolate. Soon Leavitt learned that she had no tolerance for alcohol. When she started singing every state song she knew, the bartender called a cab for her. Despite her inebriated state, she remembered to take her notebook. She slept it off.

"I still love this drink, but now I know my limit is four sips," she says.

INGREDIENTS

2 ounces vodka

1 ounce coffee-flavored liqueur

DIRECTIONS

Place the ingredients in a mixing glass filled with ice. Stir. Strain into an old-fashioned glass filled with fresh ice. Prefer a sweeter drink? Add more of the liqueur and less vodka.

61 Local

61 Bergen Street
61local.com
brooklynpoets.org
718-875-1150
Monday through Thursday, 7 a.m. to 12 a.m.
Friday, 7 a.m. to 1 a.m.
Saturday, 9 a.m. to 1 a.m.
Sunday, 9 a.m. to 12 a.m.

———————

Since 61 Local arrived on the scene in the Cobble Hill neighborhood of Brooklyn in 2010, the bar and restaurant located in an old carriage house soon became a hangout for local writers. The owners envisioned a true public house, where people from the neighborhood could gather and work at its industrial-chic bar and communal tables day and night. "It's a space for people to communicate and corroborate," says Stephanie Cohen, the front of house manager.

When authors had readings at the local indie bookstore, BookCourt (which sadly closed in December 2016), many would head two blocks away to 61 Local afterward with their friends and fellow writers for food and drink. Small literary and cultural magazines hold their launch parties here. Julia Dahl celebrated the release of her second novel, *Run You Down*, and wrote the majority of her third novel, *Conviction*, in this open

Day or night, 61 Local is always buzzing.

and inviting cafe setting. Dahl ran into writer Michele Filgate, whom she had known only via Twitter, when Dahl sat down at a table next to her's to work. Filgate "was chatting with a couple of other writers who were there doing some work, and we all ended up talking writing for almost an hour," Dahl says. "It's that kind of place."

Brooklyn Poets Yawp holds a combined poetry workshop and open mic event on the second Monday of each month in 61 Local's event space. Jason Koo, its founder and a poet, is drawn to expansive poems of consciousness and about America. Between teaching jobs, he wanted to celebrate Brooklyn poets such as Hart Crane, Marianne Moore, and onetime resident, W. H. Auden. Knowing that Brooklyn had become a literary hub for writers, Koo established the nonprofit Brooklyn Poets in 2012 on the birthday of Brooklyn's own Walt Whitman, one of Koo's favorite poets. At first, Koo and several other poets held small, intensive poetry workshops in their homes. "The community started building," Koo says. "Now it is almost like family." Koo, who had no experience starting a nonprofit organization, learned on the fly. "It was like building a poem," he says.

In April 2013, which is National Poetry Month, Koo held the first Brooklyn Poets Yawp on 61 Local's wide open, yet quiet second floor. "Yawp" comes from Verse 52 of Whitman's "Song of Myself:" "I sound my barbaric yawp over the roofs of the world." During the first hour, some 45 or so writers work on poems under the tutelage of a published poet. In the second hour, they read them to an audience of 50 to 70.

Koo, who says his soul dwells in the nineteenth century and its literature, prefers spirits of that vintage. His cocktail of choice is an Old Fashioned. Although he can't order one at 61 Local because its menu is limited to beer and wine, he can get his poetry fix there. The restaurant emphasizes local food and beer from the Northeast. However, Bloody Marys, Moscow Mules, and mimosas are featured on the brunch menu.

68 Jay Street Bar

68 Jay Street
68jaystreetbar.net
718-260-8207
Daily: 2:30 p.m. until 2 a.m.

———————————

Walt Whitman and Hart Crane ambled the streets of this part of Brooklyn on the East River and found inspiration. In 1924, Crane, then living in Columbia Heights, wrote to his mother and grandmother: "Just imagine looking out your window directly on the East River with nothing intervening between your view of the Statue of Liberty, way down the harbor, and the marvelous beauty of Brooklyn Bridge close above you on your right!" He told them of his view of Manhattan skyscrapers and the "constant stream of tugs, liners, sail boats, etc [*sic*] in procession before you on the river!"

Almost a century later, Karen Johnson, a modern dancer, arrived in the area, now called DUMBO, an acronym for Down Under the Manhattan Bridge Overpass, and found a thriving community of artists and galleries tucked in nineteenth- and twentieth-century warehouses. In 2003, Johnson and Steve West settled upon a space in the historic Grand Union tea warehouse, a nineteenth-century behemoth that occupied an entire city block in the shadows of the Brooklyn and Manhattan bridges, for their neighborhood bar. They scraped away layers of the past and found beautiful brick walls and terracotta arches. They added a reclaimed wood bar stained a warm golden color and low benches with small occasional tables. With its soft lighting and candles throughout, Johnson likens the atmosphere to an evening sitting around a campfire. Whitman would approve.

The neighborhood is filled with literary ghosts. Mere steps away was the site formerly referred to as Fulton Landing, where crowds could board one of Robert Fulton's ferries to travel to Manhattan until 1924. In the last half of the nineteenth century, Whitman witnessed the construction of that bridge from his Brooklyn Heights print shop and took the ferry daily to Manhattan, most likely for his evenings at Pfaff's. A plaque on Old Fulton Street marks the headquarters of the *Brooklyn Daily Eagle*, where Whitman worked as an editor.

In the second edition of *Leaves of Grass*, published in 1856, his poem, first called "Sun-Down Poem" and then in later revisions, "Crossing Brooklyn Ferry," appeared. Whitman writes,

> *Others will enter the gates of the ferry and cross from shore to shore,*
> *Others will watch the run of the flood-tide,*
> *Others will see the shipping of Manhattan north and west, and the*
> *heights of Brooklyn to the south and east . . .*

In later decades, Truman Capote, W. H. Auden, and Carson McCullers took up residence in the shadow of these bridges. So moved by his locale, Crane celebrated the Brooklyn Bridge in his 1933 poem, "The Bridge."

In its post-industrial age, DUMBO and bordering neighborhoods have drawn another generation of artistic souls. Fulton's Landing has since been converted to a state park; in 2006 ferry service returned. Meanwhile,

68 Jay Street has become a haunt of the staff of indie book publisher, Melville House, founded in 2001 by sculptor Valerie Merians and fiction writer/journalist Dennis Johnson, located a few blocks away. In 2006, publisher powerHouse Books set up a laboratory for creative thought and a venue for all kinds of performances, including numerous literary events and exhibitions two blocks away from 68 Jay Street, on the other side of the Manhattan Bridge. The group also operates an eclectic bookshop.

Occupants of the studios and tech companies in the warehouses, as well as in the surrounding area, have made 68 Jay Street a destination for its variety of wines and craft beers. Johnson, an oenophile, is proud of their wine selection. Although the bar has no cocktail menu, thirsty creative types may order one of the classics.

At 68 Jay Street, the mix of artists, writers, musicians, and techies make for a vibrant atmosphere, which extends to this watering hole's staff. "I am able to give a singer/songwriter a job that has allowed her to start her own American Folk Festival in Brooklyn," she says. An actor who is active in local theater and moving to film, a photographer, and a person who teaches arts to children round out her staff. "In supporting all of them, I feel I am supporting an arts scene that is more difficult to be a part of these days," Johnson says. The bar features live music on Saturday evenings.

Brooklyn Inn

148 Hoyt Street
718-522-2525
Monday through Thursday, 4 p.m. to 4 a.m.;
Friday, 3 p.m. to 4 a.m.; weekends, 2 p.m. to 4 a.m.

Brooklyn native Jonathan Lethem made the Brooklyn Inn, which first opened in 1885, his regular drinking place and set a scene in his detective novel *Motherless Brooklyn* at this landmark tavern. Lethem, who lived around the corner from the bar, chose his neighborhood, Boerum Hill, as the backdrop for this novel as well as for his novel *The Fortress of Solitude*. Lethem also spent his childhood in this six-block section of Brooklyn. He has been known to meet up with several writer friends every few months at this watering hole.

Enter the corner bar and it's easy to see why writers seek fellowship or, if they prefer, solitude, here. Despite a jukebox, Conal Darcy writes on the website Brokelyn that Brooklyn Inn is "the perfect place to tackle a heavy work like *Between the World and Me*" by Ta-Nehisi Coates, who has lived in Brooklyn since 2001. "The neighborhood is full of writers, so you might only have your reading interrupted by someone celebrating their book deal or selling a show," Darcy adds.

From its original woodwork by a Bohemian woodworker at a factory located in the Bushwick section of Brooklyn, to the vaulted tin ceilings, the place feels old world, old school—comfortable but not worn out. The saloon in its early decades catered to the working class. The original owner, a native of Germany, installed an 1870s carved wooden bar imported from his birthplace.

The well-preserved Brooklyn Inn has such allure that architect Joel Shifflet wrote a booklet on its history—after nine years of research, *Hoyt and Bergen Streets: Origins of a Brooklyn Corner Bar* is for sale at the bar. "Saloons like this were designed and built to be elegant, and the high ceiling, woodwork, stained glass, and mirror are part of creating this quality," Shifflet told the website Brownstoner in 2016. "Also, I thought the elements of the interior revealed their age and could be 'read'—that we could look at them and feel, possibly know, what people before us experienced."

During his research, Shifflet traced the meaning of the carving under the bar top, a Valknut symbol. "It is associated with the Germanic god Odin, and the three parts symbolize physical capability, inspiration, and intoxication," he says.

The bar survived Prohibition, although after one raid the doors were shuttered for eight months. In 1956, the bar was no longer run by German-Americans, changing hands several times more. The last time the bar was sold was in 1990. The once blighted neighborhood, which was designated a historic landmark in 1974, has undergone gentrification with chic cafés and high-end shops dotting its blocks.

When Jonathan Ames' HBO detective comedy *Bored to Death* was canceled in 2011, he invited his fans via Twitter to join him at the bar for a wake. He offered to buy a drink for all who showed up at 10 p.m. on a December evening. His offer attracted quite the crowd of fans, some of whom asked him to sign his novels or memoirs. "I didn't expect this turnout," Ames told a *New York Times* reporter.

Esquire drinks writer, history buff, former professor of English literature, and cocktail guru, David Wondrich, who lives in the neighborhood considers the Brooklyn Inn among his favorite places to drink, writing that the bar is "a very pleasant place to have a drink, although the jukebox isn't what it used to be." A winner of a James Beard award for his book *Imbibe!*, Wondrich told a blogger, "I'd always had a love for wet literature—things like P. G. Wodehouse and Raymond Carver where everyone was always taking a drink—and, over the years I'd collected a handful of amusing drink books." Brooklyn Inn provides the right spot for a tipple accompanied by a good read.

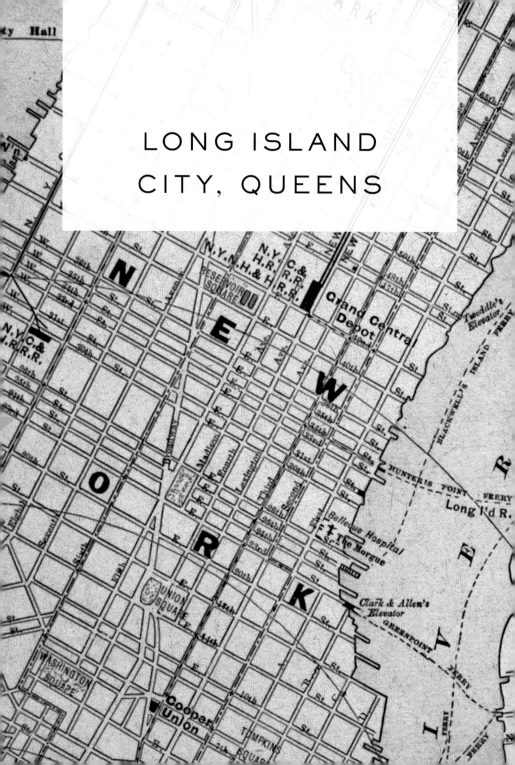

LONG ISLAND CITY, QUEENS

North of Brooklyn and across the river from Manhattan's Upper East Side, Long Island City was inhabited by a neat row houses and a mix of aging factories on the East River until about two decades ago. Its waterfront area, formerly clotted with aging storage houses, factories, and taxi depots, has undergone quite a face-lift. Its waterfront, across from Midtown Manhattan and the United Nations, has risen out of urban blight to become a trendy hot spot, with tall, glass-covered skyscrapers and hot bars and restaurants. A Silvercup sign atop the former commercial bakery, with its red light, can be seen from Manhattan day and night. The building has been transformed into TV studios. While some factories remain active, this part of Long Island City has attracted artists, galleries, and museums.

The Queensboro Bridge, which is memorialized in Simon and Garfunkel's "59th Street Bridge," begins in Manhattan and ends here. Novelists have used the bridge in their plots for various reasons. "The city seen from the Queensboro Bridge is always the city seen for the first time, in its wild promise of all the mystery and the beauty in the world," observes Nick Carraway as he and Jay Gatsby cross the bridge for drinks in Manhattan. The principal character in Truman Capote's *Summer Crossing*, published posthumously in 2005, steers her car skidding onto the bridge, taking her three passengers on a fatal ride. When one of her passengers cries, "Damn it, you'll kill us," she replies, "I know"—the last words of the novel.

This triangular section of Queens, in the shadows of the bridge, has become a hot spot for an active literary community as well. LIC resident Julie Powell cooked her way through Julia Child's oeuvre and became a best-selling author. Jessica Valenti, author and founder of the blog *Feministing*, grew up in Long Island City. The group Astoria Writers Write(!) meets each week for three hours of schmoozing, writing sessions, and critiques in a restaurant in Astoria, which borders Long Island City to the east.

LIC Bar

45-58 Vernon Boulevard
licbar.com
licreadingseries.com
718-786-5400
Weekdays: 4 p.m. to 4 a.m.
Saturday: 1 p.m. to 4 a.m.
Sunday: 1 p.m. to midnight

———————————

Running parallel to the East River, the somewhat less gentrified Vernon Boulevard is lined with trendy restaurants, bars, and cafes, all dishing out many of the world's cuisines and serving up classic and contemporary libations. In the heart of the neighborhood sits the LIC Bar, a bar that dates to 1929.

Writer/sculptor Catherine LaSota, who moved into the neighborhood and became a regular, proposed the reading series to the bar owner. She was steeped in New York's literary scene, attending readings in Brooklyn and Manhattan, but found nothing similar in her new surroundings. The reading series, inaugurated in 2015, takes place in the carriage house in the backyard, away from the noise of the bar. The owner transformed it into a performance space. In the winter, the stone fireplace in the corner is ablaze in this brick-walled room.

On the second Tuesday of each month, three authors read from their latest novels, short story collections, or memoirs. In the audience may

be fellow authors such as Rachel Cantor, Dylan Landis, Valerie Keane, and Rob Spillman, the editor of the literary magazine *Tin House*. After two authors read, the audience may buy drinks and mingle. The intimate space allows authors to connect with their readership, LaSota notes.

Following intermission, the final author reads, and then LaSota leads a panel discussion with the authors about their writing process. She has each one share a personal anecdote about Queens. Audience members write their questions on slips of paper. The lucky ones whose questions are drawn receive a gift certificate from a local Queens business. At the end of the evening, people can buy the authors' books, which are sold by Astoria Bookshop on-site, and have them signed. Many of the guests and authors linger for a few hours. That night's authors may not have met before, but friendships often form by the end of the evening.

"The literary world is one of the most supportive of the creative fields," LaSota says. "It's a really good feeling. Maybe it's because we spend so much time alone. It's fun to get together at these reading series."

The diverse series has showcased Rumaan Alam, Amy Brill, Robin Black, Cantor, Tobias Carroll, Alexander Chee, Julia Fierro, Phil Klay, John Leguizamo, Sara Nović, Sam Lipsyte, Paul Lisicky, Patrick Ryan, and Lynn Steger Strong.

The bar also hosts an official "Bookend Event" during the Brooklyn Book Festival.

Scotch lovers will appreciate this bar's deep selection of Scotch.

THE LAST WORD

Not only is Catherine LaSota the founder of the LIC Bar reading series, she worked as a bartender for six years, although not at the LIC. A musician, she also likes to perform and says this series brings together three things she loves.

Although this gin-based drink rose to popularity during Prohibition, one cocktail historian uncovered evidence of its existence in 1916. The Last Word was listed on the Detroit Athletic Club's menu three years before the Volstead Act was passed. The cocktail disappeared from bar menus for several decades until Seattle bartender Murray Stenson came across it in 2004 in *Ted Saucier's Bottoms Up!*, a 1951 cocktail book. Stenson introduced the cocktail to a new generation of drinkers. From there, its popularity spread from the Pacific Northwest to the East Coast.

"It's the perfect combination if sweet and tangy, and it packs a good punch while going down easily—much like the experience of reading a really great book," LaSota says. "As a huge fan of literature, I can't help but love the name of this cocktail."

This cocktail goes well with short story collections or the works of Franz Kafka, beloved by LaSota. "He'll never be in the reading series, but I love his work," she says.

INGREDIENTS

1 ounce green chartreuse

1 ounce gin

1 ounce Luxardo (maraschino liqueur)

1 ounce fresh lime juice

DIRECTIONS

Add all ingredients to an ice-filled cocktail shaker. Shake vigorously and serve in a chilled coupe glass.

SELECTED BIBLIOGRAPHY

Angoff, Charles. *H. L. Mencken: A Portrait from Memory*. New York: American Book-Stratford Press, 1956.

Benchley, Nathaniel. *Robert Benchley: A Biography*. New York: McGraw-Hill, 1955.

Broyard, Anatole. *Kafka Was the Rage: A Greenwich Village Memoir*. New York: Random House, 1997.

Callow, Philip. *From Noon to Starry Night: A Life of Walt Whitman*. Chicago: Ivan R. Dee, Inc., 1992.

Case, Frank. *Do Not Disturb*. New York: J. B. Lipincott, 1940.

Churchill, Allen. *The Improper Bohemians*. New York: E. P. Dutton, 1959.

———. *The Literary Decade*. Englewood Cliffs, NJ: Prentice-Hall, 1971.

———. *Park Row*. New York: Rinehart & Co.

Clarke, Helen Marie. *Over P.J. Clarke's Bar: Tales from New York City's Famous Saloon*. New York: Skyhorse Publishing, 2012.

Edmiston, Susan, and Linda C. Cirino. *Literary New York: A History and Guide*. Layton, UT: Gibbs-Smith, 1991.

Gaines, James R. *Wit's End: Days and Nights of the Algonquin Round Table.* New York: Harvest/Harcourt Brace Jovanovich, 1977.

Gill, Brendan. *Here at The New Yorker.* New York: Random House, 1975.

Hirschfeld, Al, and Gordon Kahn. *The Speakeasies of 1932.* Milwaukee: Glenn Young Books/Applause, 2003.

Hughes, Evan. *Literary Brooklyn: The Writers of Brooklyn and the Story of American City Life.* New York: Henry Holt and Company, 2011.

Kaytor, Marilyn. *"21": The Life and Times of New York's Favorite Club.* New York: Viking Press, 1975.

Kriendler, H. Peter, with H. Paul Jeffers. *"21": Every Day Was New Year's Eve.* New York: Taylor Trade Publishing, 1999.

Lerner, Michael A. *Dry Manhattan: Prohibition in New York City.* Cambridge, MA: Harvard University Press, 2007.

Martin, Justin. *Rebel Souls: Walt Whitman and America's First Bohemians.* Boston: Da Capo Press, 2014.

Meade, Marion. *Bobbed Hair and Bathtub Gin: Writers Running Wild in the Twenties.* New York: Harcourt, 2004.

———. *Dorothy Parker: What Fresh Hell is This?* New York: Penguin, 1989.

Miles, Barry. *Ginsberg: A Biography.* New York: Simon & Schuster, 1989.

Miller, Terry. *Greenwich Village and How It Got That Way.* New York: Crown, 1990.

Mitchell, Joseph. *Up in the Old Hotel.* New York: Vintage/Random House, 1993.

Morgan, Bill. *Literary Landmarks of New York.* New York: Universe Publishing, 2002.

Morley, Christopher. *Christopher Morley's New York.* New York: Fordham University Press, 1988.

Morris, Jan. *Manhattan '45*. London: Faber and Faber, 2011.

Morris, Lloyd. *Incredible New York: High Life and Low Life from 1850 to 1950*. Syracuse, NY: Syracuse University Press, 1996.

Laing, Olivia. *The Trip to Echo Springs: On Writers and Drinking*. New York: Picador, 2014.

Sexton, Andrea Wyatt, and Alice Leccesse Powers, eds. *The Brooklyn Reader: Thirty Writers Celebrate America's Favorite Borough*. New York: Crown Publishers, 1994.

Simon, Kate. *New York Places & Pleasures*. New York: Meridian Books, 1960.

Sismondo, Christine. *America Walks into a Bar: A Spirited History of Taverns and Saloons, Speakeasies and Grog Shops*. New York: Oxford University Press, 2011.

Smith, Patti. *Just Kids*. New York: Ecco, 2010.

Strausbaugh, John. *The Village: 400 Years of Beats and Bohemians, Radicals and Rogues*. New York: Ecco, 2013.

Tippins, Sherill. *Inside the Dream Palace: The Life and Times of New York's Legendary Chelsea Hotel*. New York: Houghton Mifflin Harcourt, 2013.

The Vault at Pfaff"'s. https://pfaffs.web.lehigh.edu/node/38094 Eds. Edward Whitley and Rob Weidman. August 7, 2016.

Wakefield, Dan. *New York in the '50s*. New York: Houghton Mifflin, 1992.

Wetzstein, Ross. *Republic of Dreams: Greenwich Village: The American Bohemia, 1910–1960*. New York: Simon & Schuster, 2002.

White, Norval, and Elliott Willensky with Fran Leadon. *AIA Guide to New York City, Fifth Edition*. New York: Oxford University Press, 2010.

The WPA Guide to New York City: The Federal Writers Project Guide to 1930s New York. New York: Random House, 1939.

ACKNOWLEDGMENTS

This book was borne out of another book idea that my sharp literary agent, Jean Sagendorph, shopped around a few years ago. No one bit because cocktail books had peaked. Noting a new uptick in interest in such books in 2016, however, Jean sent my proposal out again. A wise woman, that one. Because of her endeavors, I have yet to touch the ground since she snagged this deal for me.

Ann Treistman, editorial director of The Countryman Press, passed on that proposal, but she didn't say no, either. She and her team suggested that I write this book instead. After sleeping on it, I woke up the next morning realizing that this book suited me even better. I am a native New Yorker who has soaked in the city's history, literary and otherwise, inhaled fiction and nonfiction books about my hometown, visited famous authors' residences, and had cocktails at the bars famous authors frequented because I am a biblio-stalker. Every time I visit the city, I can never leave it without buying a book. Ann and the team at The Countryman Press, thank you for coming up with the concept for this book.

Dan Crissman, my editor, helped me shape this book, providing editorial insight and support. I am so fortunate that he had my back and walked me through the process from book idea to finished book. His editorial assistant, Michael Tizzano, helped at every stage. Go, Terriers, Michael! Richard Beck, your queries and edits were invaluable in sharpening my sentences and content. You pointed the way when my sentences strayed. Thank you, Devorah Backman, for helping me navigate around the world of book promotion.

To everyone else at The Countryman Press and W. W. Norton, I greatly appreciate having your marketing and publishing savvy on my team.

My research took me on epic literary pub crawls through New York City. In a two-and-a-half-day period, I racked up nearly 30 miles, according to my pedometer. On another, a marathon's worth. I visited all of these bars (as well as, in two cases, their former addresses), attended readings, and interviewed so many people. My gratitude to Flerine Atienza and Tommy Warren, Frank Caiafa, Rachel Cantor, Alexander Chee, Patrick Daley and Adriane Kufta, Christopher Dorsey, Claudia Dreifus, Avery Fletcher and Christopher Rivera, Tad Friend, Christopher Green, John Hague, Kevin Cole, Sebastian Junger, Catherine LaSota, Caroline Leavitt, Michael Long, Karim Karouni, Gerard Meagher, Austin Nixon, Sylvia Paret, Bill Potter, Adam Rogers, Erika Robuck, Jessica Rosen and Alessandro Borgognone, Penina Roth, Nicholas Sciammarella, Lindsey Sawyer and Phil Scotti, Isabel Costa-Chan and Ashley Kalstek, J. Courtney Sullivan, Lisa Kristel, Jason Koo, Karen Johnson, Stephanie Cohen, and Denis Woychuk.

I am indebted to the vast resources at the main branch of the New York Public Library, one of New York's crown jewels, and at new and used book dealers everywhere.

As a child, I yearned to be Harriet the Spy when I grew up. I too wished to wander the streets of Manhattan with a black-marbled composition book, taking notes about the city's people and sights. I became a journalist. With this book, I lived the dream. (I also fantasized about sleeping overnight at the Metropolitan Museum of Art after reading *From the Mixed-up Files of Mrs. Basil E. Frankweiler.* I've yet to cross that one off my list.) Thank you, Louise Fitzhugh, for creating a character that has stayed with me all my life.

To my family, friends, and my followers on Facebook and Twitter, many of whom are fellow writers, journalists, bookworms, and authors, I appreciate your enthusiastic support all these many years. Erin McHugh and Bethanne Patrick, I'm thrilled we made the Round Table redux happen. Meeting and making new writer friends made me feel less alone in my writerly pursuits.

Meta and Susan, you two keep me sane. (I know. That seems like a stretch.) Both of you have been loyal friends through thick and thin, sometimes lubricated with gin and tonics. We are GGs forever.

Sasha, your dedication and passion for music and your success as a guitarist are an inspiration to me.

No way could I have done this without Rob, my husband and also a writer. His enthusiasm and unwavering support for my work has no bounds. As my deadline approached, I would have starved had it not been for his chefly talents, best limited to picking up takeout. We've never had pitchers of martinis like Nick and Nora do in *The Thin Man*, much less in the middle of the night, but we share their wit and zaniness. Nevertheless, I love exploring our native New York City with him, seeking out its hidden gems, hanging out for hours in bookstores, and ending our days feasting on cocktails and oysters. I'll be seeing you. Always.

INDEX

ABOUT THE AUTHOR

Delia Cabe has written for *Self*, *Prevention*, *Health*, *The Boston Globe Magazine*, *Boston Magazine*, *Scientific American Presents*, and other newspapers and magazines. An avid gardener, she lives in a Boston suburb with her husband, Rob, and their two cats. She teaches magazine and column writing at Emerson College.